Life After Victoria
1900–1909

Life After Victoria

1900–1909

The Decade Series

Alison Maloney
Jim Maloney

REMEMBER WHEN

First published in Great Britain in 2008 by
Remember When
An imprint of
Pen & Sword Books Ltd
47 Church Street
Barnsley
South Yorkshire
S70 2AS

ISBN 978 1 84468 035 1

A CIP catalogue record for this book is available from the British Library

Typeset by Phoenix Typesetting, Auldgirth, Dumfriesshire
Printed and bound by CPI UK

Pen & Sword Books Ltd incorporates the Imprints of Pen & Sword Aviation, Pen & Sword Maritime, Pen & Sword Military, Wharncliffe Local History, Pen & Sword Select, Pen & Sword Military Classics, Leo Cooper, Remember When, Seaforth Publishing and Frontline Publishing

For a complete list of Pen & Sword titles please contact
PEN & SWORD BOOKS LIMITED
47 Church Street, Barnsley, South Yorkshire, S70 2AS, England
E-mail: enquiries@pen-and-sword.co.uk
Website: www.pen-and-sword.co.uk

For Georgia and Joe
who may find this useful in later years

Contents

Contents

Contents

Introduction

Although Queen Victoria was still on the throne at the turn of the century, her demise, in January 1901, ushered in the bright, optimistic Edwardian era. The decade over which Victoria's son, Edward VII, was to rule saw massive changes which would affect every aspect of daily life.

The Boer War was soon to draw to a close and the First World War was still a long way off; houses were becoming brighter and less oppressive, and technology in transport and industry was advancing in leaps and bounds. According to historian Samuel Hynes, it was a 'leisurely time, when women wore picture hats and did not vote, when the rich were not ashamed to live conspicuously, and the sun really never set on the British flag'.

Undoubtedly, the age was golden for the middle and upper classes but there was still a great deal of inequality and grinding poverty. Nonetheless, by the end of the decade, many laws to alleviate the dire circumstances of the poor were beginning to reach the statute books and women were beginning to see tiny but significant concessions towards equal rights.

Life After Victoria, for most, brought a new dawn and a feeling of hope for the future.

Chapter One

1900

Politics

CREATION OF THE LABOUR PARTY

HISTORY WAS made at the Memorial Hall in London's Farringdon Street, when 129 delegates from 65 trade unions and three Socialist societies met to establish a Labour group in Parliament to campaign for workers' rights.

They passed a motion by Scottish miner James Keir Hardie to form 'a distinct Labour group in Parliament, who shall have their own whips, and agree upon their policy, which must embrace a readiness to cooperate with any party which for the time being may be engaged in promoting legislation in the direct interests of labour'.

Calling themselves, the 'Labour Representation Committee', James Ramsay MacDonald was voted secretary.

Hardie later made the poetic remark, 'It has come. Poor little child of danger, nursling of the storm. May it be blessed.'

The LRC put up 15 candidates in the 1900 General Election, winning 62,698 votes. Two of the candidates, Keir Hardie and Richard Bell, won seats in the House of Commons.

The LRC was to change its name in 1906 to the Labour Party.

Scottish miner, Keir Hardie, was one of the founding fathers of what is now known as the Labour Party.

Boer War hero and war correspondent,
Winston Churchill became an MP.

WINSTON CHURCHILL BECOMES MP

Winston Churchill, who had failed to be elected as Conservative MP for Oldham in 1899, returned a year later to stand again in the general election. This time he succeeded.

The 26-year-old son of Tory politician Lord Randolph Churchill capitalised on his privileged upbringing. Educated at Harrow, he attended Sandhurst Royal Military College, after which he saw service in India and the Sudan. Churchill made a name for himself during this time by also acting as a war correspondent.

He left the Army in 1899 to take up politics, but first travelled to South Africa as a journalist. Taken prisoner by the Boers, he made a daring escape and returned home to a hero's welcome. The nation warmed to some stirring patriotic news after a string of failures for the British Army against the Boers. His fame helped him to win his parliamentary seat as the member for Oldham.

UNREST IN IRELAND

Irish Nationalist leader John Redmond called for an uprising against the British.

Royalty

ASSASSINATION ATTEMPT ON PRINCE OF WALES

The Prince of Wales escaped uninjured when a 15-year old anarchist fired at him on a train as it left a railway station in Brussels. Jean-Baptiste Sipido stepped onto the footboard of the train, which was taking the Prince and the Princess on a trip to Copenhagen.

An attempt to assassinate the Prince of Wales, later Edward VII, was foiled on 4th April, 1900.

He pointed the gun at the Prince through the window and fired twice but missed his target. He was quickly apprehended and found to be carrying anarchist literature.

Brussels was a centre of opposition to the British role in the Boer War at this time, and Sipido told police he wanted to kill the Prince who had so many men killed in South Africa.

FIRE AND WATER

There were red faces all around as the new Royal Yacht, *Victoria and Albert*, capsized as it left the port of Southampton. Later in the year, a fire at Buckingham Palace destroyed part of the roof.

ITALIAN KING MURDERED

King Umberto I of Italy was assassinated by anarchist Gaetano Bresci in Monza, near Milan on July 30. He was shot three times.

The King had become deeply unpopular with many for his ruthlessness. During the colonial wars in Africa, there were large demonstrations at home over the rising price of bread. The city of Milan was put under the military control of General Fiorenzo Bava-Beccaris, who ordered the use of cannons on the demonstrators.

Over a hundred died and a thousand were wounded. The King outraged a great many of his people by sending a telegram to the General congratulating him for restoring order.

Bresci said he killed the King because he wanted to avenge the people killed by Bava-Beccaris.

King Umberto was succeeded by his son, Victor Emmanuel III.

BIRTHS

August 4 – Elizabeth Bowes-Lyon, The Queen Mother.
June 25 – Lord (Louis) Mountbatten, son of Prince Louis of Battenberg, who became British military commander and last Viceroy of India.

Historical Events

BOER WAR

After the outbreak of hostilities the previous October, the British suffered a series of defeats at the hands of the Boers in South Africa.

In January, Field Marshall Lord Roberts arrived in Cape Town to assume supreme command of the British forces and in February, the turn around began. After 118 days, the siege of garrison town, Ladysmith, ended when a relief column of cavalry arrived and the Boers packed their wagons and retreated.

In May, the seven-month siege of Mafeking, the small town on the railway line to Rhodesia, was lifted after British troops arrived.

When the Boers surrendered the Orange Free State and the Transvaal to the British, it was the beginning of the end.

In September, Lord Roberts declared that the war was over, but scattered fighting continued and the war was not officially ended until two years later.

BOXER REBELLION

The Boxer Rebellion against foreign influence in China, which started in November of the previous year, escalated to alarming proportions.

The Boxers, who called themselves 'Fists of Righteous Harmony', began as members of a patriotic society devoted to martial arts. But it turned into

The bloody Boer War was declared over in 1900 but sporadic fighting continued until 1902 when it was officially over. Over 20,000 British troops died in the fighting with a further 22,829 injured.

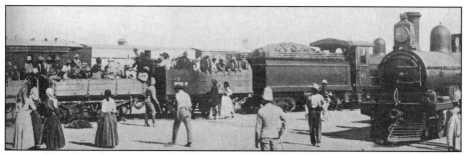

The nation celebrated when the siege of Mafeking was finally over. It was seen as a turning point in the war and filled the front pages of the newspapers, including this 19th May entry from *The Daily Mail.*

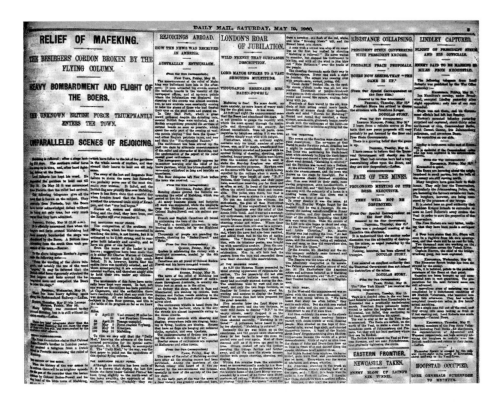

a popular movement against foreign and Christian influence in their country. They were joined by disaffected soldiers and some high officials in the Manchu regime.

In June 1900, the Boxers, some 140,000 strong, invaded Peking, killing hundreds of foreigners, including the hated missionaries and Chinese Christians. Thousands more were killed throughout China.

Many women and children took refuge in the British Embassy which came under heavy attack. After eight weeks, the siege was lifted by an international force of British, French, Russian, American, German, and Japanese troops.

Despite their defeat, the Boxers carried on fighting, but the uprising had been crushed.

BIRTHS

October 7 – Heinrich Himmler, German Nazi and SS chief.

Social Change

During the reign of Queen Victoria, UK cities, especially London, had become hugely overcrowded, leaving the poorer classes crammed into sub-standard accommodation. Slums had sprung up all over the country and one rented room often housed a whole family, if not two.

The luckier workers had houses built for them by the factory owner or landowner, but even these were often just two rooms, one upstairs and one downstairs. With the average Victorian couple having four or five children, the family home was a crowded place.

Houses had no running water and no bathrooms and the water from the communal pump was often unclean. Worse still, some of the 'back to backs' had a sewer running through the street and this poor sanitation meant many children didn't make it to adulthood.

By 1900, many slums had been demolished but, for the very poor, that only meant having to move from one hovel to another.

INFLUENZA HITS THE UK

Despite Louis Pasteur's discovery of bacteria in 1867, medical knowledge was poor and disease spread quickly through the crowded slums. New treatments for Cholera, Typhoid, Scarlet Fever and Tuberculosis (TB) were beginning to have a limited impact but these diseases still claimed many lives.

In January, an influenza epidemic in London claimed 50 lives a day and other major UK cities were also hit. Gravediggers and undertakers struggled to cope with the demand and, due to a shortage of nurses, hospitals were forced to turn patients away.

Later in the year, bubonic plague swept through Glasgow.

SOCIAL JUSTICE FOR CHILDREN

The battle for social reforms had made huge progress during the Victorian era, and by 1900 it was illegal for children under 11 to work, as had been the norm 50 years ago.

Thanks to an act passed in 1870, it was compulsory for all children under 14 to receive an education. School varied from the academic – where reading, writing and arithmetic were the top subjects – to the industrial, where youngsters learned a skill such as carpentry or lacemaking. 'Half-time' schools were also set up for those children who were already in employment, to help them study in their spare time.

Fashion

The Twentieth Century saw a sweeping change in the nature of fashion. As the new decade dawned, fashionable clothes were the preserve of the wealthy and influential. The less affluent could only dream of such a luxury. Further industrialisation and an increase in global transport meant that the relative cost of clothes dropped dramatically throughout the century. Fashion was set to become the domain of all walks of society.

Although Queen Victoria was still on the throne, fashion was already into its 'Edwardian' era, particularly when it came to the female silhouette. A new corset introduced in 1900 dramatically altered the figure into an 'S' shape, forcing the bosom

Fashion owed nothing to nature when it came to women's figures and corsetry.

forward and the hips back, giving the appearance of a large chest and bottom.

Surprisingly, this constricting undergarment was dubbed the 'health corset' and was thought to benefit the wearer by removing the pressure exerted by conventional corsets on the waist and diaphragm. Invented by French lady Mme Gaches-Sarraute, who had studied medicine, the corset was believed to mirror the natural curves of a woman's body, while freeing up the bust and extending further down the hips. Laced too tightly, however, it produced the extraordinary 'S' line, or 'Kangaroo Stance' that is characteristic of the early part of the decade.

For the affluent lady, there were still many layers of clothing to contend with at the end of the Victorian era. As well as the corset, there was the chemise, the corset cover, several petticoats in flannel, cotton and silk and finally, the gown. Considering the more elegant ladies changed their outfit up to five times a day, it's surprising they had time to do anything else!

While the upper echelons of society were setting the trends, the ladies of the increasingly prosperous middle classes (spurred on by the popular fashion magazines showing the latest designs from Paris) spent much time and energy attempting to keep up. Dressmakers were often employed to replicate the beautiful creations sold by the fashion houses of Paris and London.

At the turn of the century, Paris fashion houses were already the acknowledged leaders of the industry. The Great Exhibition, where designers such as Doucet, the Callot Soeurs and English houses Redfern and Worth displayed their wares, confirmed the city's status further. Mme Paquin, the first successful woman in *haute couture*, drew gasps of admiration with her contribution – a wax model of herself in one of her own creations.

But in the decade ahead, more and more Paris designers, including Mme Paquin, opened branches in London, making up-to-the-minute designs available to the affluent English rose.

Entertainment

HOME ENTERTAINMENT

With no TV or radio, most evenings revolved around conversation, reading and games. For those who could afford the instruments, music was an option and for the very wealthy there was a new, hi-tech form of home entertainment available:

The 'electrophone' was a telephone-based service that gave people access to concerts in the comfort of their own homes. Subscribers could hear music, theatrical performances and even sermons, at home or at special listening-in points. This early precursor to radio was quite expensive and was scrapped in the 1920s.

THEATRE

West End plays and operas were a popular pastime for the well to do, but many theatres in the late Victorian era were given over to music halls and 'spectacles', where paranormal events, such as hypnotists, mediums and ghost conjurers were the entertainment. Magic shows and circus acts were immensely popular.

On January 15, the Hippodrome theatre opened on the corner of Charing Cross Road and Cranbourn Street in London. Designed by Frank Matcham, it was originally built as a Hippodrome for circuses, and it housed a vast tank for water spectacles. It was not until 1909 that the stage was extended to accommodate variety acts and, later, revues.

For children, theatre began on Boxing Day with the arrival of the pantomime season. The traditional pantomime included a harlequinade, with a mysterious Harlequin, a beautiful Columbine and a jolly clown, but by the end of the Victorian era, this feature was cut down to the closing comic turn – if not eliminated. The Christmas show in 1900 would not differ greatly to the ones our children watch today.

On May 4, the celebrated beauty, Mrs Lillie Langtry, took her portrayal of a dissolute courtesan in *The Degenerates* to Washington. She was an instant sensation, packing the theatre there as she had in London.

Lillie Langtry, the darling of the stage – and the Prince of Wales – performed in Washington to critical acclaim.

Also in the States, *Floradora* opened at Broadway's Casino Theatre. It introduced dancing girls called *The Floradora Sextet*, a precursor to the chorus line.

Puccini's *Tosca* was premiered in Rome. The story of the singer who offers herself to a villainous police chief to save her lover's life, aroused much passion in the opera loving audience.

On November 22, Sir Arthur Sullivan, one half of Gilbert and Sullivan, died at the age of 58. His collaboration with W.S.Gilbert, which had begun 25 years earlier, had produced 13 hit operettas, including the hugely popular *HMS Pinafore* and *The Mikado,* and had ensured packed houses at the specially built Savoy theatre in London. Sadly, the pair fell out over the price of a carpet for the theatre in 1890 and, although they were reconciled three years later, subsequent works flopped.

FILM

Four years before the turn of the century, on February 20, 1896, the first British cinema audience had gathered at The Regent Street Polytechnic in London to watch short films by French pioneers, the Lumiere Brothers. By 1900, films were being shown as part of the evening's entertainment at music halls up and down the country. As they were silent, they were usually accompanied by a pianist, although a new innovation in France was about to change that. In April, the moving picture acquired sound with the use of a phonograph beside the screen, controlled by the projectionist. For the first time, a private viewer could hear as well as see an artist on the screen.

Also in France, the Lumiere Brothers premiered their new wide-screen format at the 1900 World Fair. At 75 mm wide, it has held the record for over 100 years as the widest format ever developed.

Films released this year included *Sherlock Holmes Baffled*, a 30 second feature shown in arcades, which was the earliest use of Conan Doyle's famous detective on screen.

BIRTHS

February 22 – screenwriter and director Luis Buñuel.
April 5 – actor Spencer Tracy.
June 6 –Arthur Askey, British comedian.
October 9 – actor Alistair Sim.
October 10 – actress Helen Hayes.
December 6 – actress Agnes Moorehead.

DEATHS

Nov 22 – Sir Arthur Sullivan, composer.

Literature

Journalist L Frank Baum created *The Wonderful Wizard of Oz*. The book was a bestseller for two years and spawned a hit stage production in 1902, which used the shorter, more familiar title, of *The Wizard of Oz*. The production started in Chicago then moved to Broadway, where it played for 293 nights from January to October 1903. Baum went on to write over 60 novels, 13 of which were sequels to Dorothy's original adventure.

In February, Winston Spencer Churchill published his first and only novel, *Savrola*. Serving as a soldier and war correspondent in the Boer War, he somehow managed to find time to pen a 70,000-word romance set against the turbulent political backdrop of a Mediterranean republic.

Other literary works published in 1900 include Anthon Chekhov's *Uncle Vanya*, Joseph Conrad's *Lord Jim* and Jerome K. Jerome's *Three Men on the Brummel*, in the long-awaited sequel to the 1889 bestseller *Three Men in a Boat*.

On November 30, the world lost a literary giant in disgraced playwright Oscar Wilde, who died in exile in Paris. The Irish writer had been living there, under the name of Sebastian Melmoth, since his release from prison (where he served two years for homosexual offences). Convicted in 1895, Wilde had written *The Ballad of Reading Gaol* while serving his sentence and it was published under the pseudonym C.33, his prison number. But his career was over. His stage successes, such as *The Importance of Being Earnest*, were unperformed since his disgrace and he died in poverty, dependent on the charity of his friends.

US writer Margaret Mitchell was born on November 8 in Atlanta, Georgia. She would grow up to write the Pulitzer Prize-winning novel, *Gone with the Wind,* while convalescing from a foot injury in 1926. The bestseller, set during and after the American Civil War, would become one of the century's most successful films in 1939. It was the only book Mitchell ever wrote. Ten years later, she was killed by a speeding taxi.

BIRTHS

June 29 – Antoine de Saint-Exupéry, novelist.
July 24 – Zelda Fitzgerald, wife and inspiration of F. Scott Fitzgerald.
November 8 – Margaret Mitchell, author.
November 19 – Anna Seghers, novelist.
December 16 – V. S. Pritchett, short story writer.

DEATHS

January 29 – John Ruskin, critic.
January 31 – John Sholto Douglas, 9th Marquess of Queensberry, (nemesis of Oscar Wilde).
November 30 – Oscar Wilde, poet and dramatist.

Architecture

THE VICTORIAN HOTCHPOTCH

The industrial revolution had an unfortunate effect on architecture and town planning in the Nineteenth Century. The shift in employment from agriculture to the manufacturing industry meant that towns had to expand quickly and, with no building regulations to speak of, this was achieved by erecting street after street of small, dingy dwellings. The fields around manufacturing towns disappeared in a flurry of development, and rural areas around mines were eaten up by the construction of grim villages.

THE ARTS AND CRAFTS MOVEMENT

In the mid-Nineteenth Century, designer William Morris began to have a huge influence on architecture. Horrified by the sub-standard materials used to build the hastily built houses of the era, he was at the forefront of the Arts and Crafts movement, along with architect Robert Norman Shaw. From the 1870s to the 1900s, Shaw changed the face of the family home by building large, spacious, well-designed homes. His country houses steered clear of the Neo-Gothic style popular with Victorians and brought back inglenook fireplaces, hanging tiles and half timber frames. He also introduced the large, open sitting rooms, with staircases running up the side, that became a feature of many mass produced homes at the turn of the century.

The Arts and Crafts movement dominated the era as artists such as William Morris and John Ruskin returned to traditional methods in an industrial age. Copper was a popular material of the style (Courtesy of Cheffins Auctioneers).

ART NOUVEAU

By 1900, Art Nouveau was gaining popularity in Europe and the Great Exhibition (Exposition Universalle) in Paris launched it as the latest style in architecture. Named after L'Art Nouveau, a progressive art gallery opened by Siegfried Bing in 1895, the new movement embraced the idea that a building, its interior design and its furnishings were parts of the same work of art and should be unified in design.

The leading exponent of Art Nouveau architecture in the UK was Charles Rennie Mackintosh, whose buildings in and around Glasgow blended the traditional Scottish crafts with the pleasing details of the new style. In 1900, he triumphed at the Eighth Secession Exhibition, Vienna, where he won great critical acclaim for his designs.

NOTABLE BUILDINGS

The building now known as the Oxo Tower, on London's South Bank, was completed, albeit without its famous tower. Originally a power station for the Post Office, it was later bought by Leibig Extract of Meat Company,

The famous Art Nouveau signs for the Paris Metro were designed by Hector Guimard.

who made the famous stock cubes. When the company redesigned the building in the 1920s, they were banned from advertising their product with illuminated signs, so the tower was built with a set of vertically aligned windows on each side, which happened to be in the shape of a circle, a cross and a circle – spelling the word OXO.

In Paris, the exhibition saw the construction of The Gare d'Orsay, now the famous Musee d'Orsay, by Victor Laloux, and the opening of the Metro, with entrances designed by Hector Guimard.

Art

Victorian art had been dominated by the Pre-Raphaelite movement led by Rosetti, Millais and William Holman Hunt. Members of the Pre-Raphaelite Brotherhood, formed in 1848, signed all their painting 'PRB' and were a huge influence on the later artists William Morris and Edward Burne-Jones. But by 1900, the tide had already begun to turn and impressionism, a movement led by Parisian artists such as Cezanne, Renoir and Monet, was gaining in popularity in the UK.

JOHN RUSKIN

On January 20, British art critic John Ruskin, died at Coniston in the Lake District. During his lifetimem, his essays on art and architecture had been

Art Nouveau poster for the 1900 Exposition Universalle Internationalle, the style which dominated the event.

Stunning Art Nouveau medal awarded to winning exhibitors at the 1900 Paris Expo.

hugely influential and often controversial. One such work flew in the face of popular opinion by stating that Turner and other landscape artists were superior to the Old Masters. He also defended the Pre-Raphaelite painters when they were scorned by art aficionados.

THE PARIS EXHIBITION

The 1900 Exposition Universalle was a massive celebration of the achievements of the Nineteenth Century and a chance to look forward to the next. Opened on April 14 by the French President M. Loubet, the ambitious exhibition covered 547 acres and, in the seven months it was open, attracted 76,000 exhibitors and 50 million members of the public.

The biggest art movement at the event was Art Noveau, characterised by bold floral designs and stylised curved shapes.

Sculptor Auguste Rodin caused a sensation when he set up his own pavilion to display his life's work, including one of his most famous scultures, *The Kiss*. The exhibition led to a surge in popularity for the sculptor and a flurry of commissions, among them an order for a replica of *The Kiss* for eccentric collector Edward Perry Warren, who lived in Lewes in Sussex. The contract for the commission, which was to cost 20,000 francs, stated that 'the genitals of the man must be complete.'

Other works of note produced this year included Edward Munch's *Red Virginia Creeper* and Thomas Eakins' *The Thinker: Portrait of Louis N. Kenton.*

Named after German Count, Ferdinand von Zeppelin, who helped to pioneer the rigid aircraft, Zeppelins offered commercial flights and were the precursor to aeroplanes.

Travel and Transport

ZEPPELIN BALLOON

Count Ferdinand von Zeppelin amazed a crowd of onlookers who had gathered to see his huge airship take to the sky for the first time.

It was 420ft long and 38ft in diameter, constructed from a wire-braced aluminium hull covered with a cotton cloth, and had a row of 16 gas cells, each filled with hydrogen. Two 16-horse-power engines gave it a potential speed of 14 mph.

Passengers, crew, and engine were carried in two aluminium gondolas suspended below.

The LZ1 made its maiden flight on July 2 at Lake Constance, near Friedrichshafen, in Southern Germany. It carried five people, attained an altitude of 1300 ft and flew a distance of 3.75 miles in 17 minutes.

THE WRIGHT BROTHERS

In September, brothers Orville and Wilbur Wright flew their 'No. 1' model, first as a kite, then as a glider.

Wilbur had watched how birds changed the angle of the ends of their wings to make their bodies roll right or left, and thought that a flying machine should try to emulate that. At the time, most of his peers thought in terms of keeping the aircraft essentially level when flying.

In 1900 the brothers journeyed to Kitty Hawk, North Carolina, to begin their manned gliding experiments. The biplane, with its 17ft wingspan, was first flown as a kite, not far above the ground, with men below holding tether ropes.

Later, Wilbur climbed on board and flew – gliding without the constraints of a tether – as much as 300 to 400ft for up to 15 seconds.

STICK CONTROL

Russian aviation pioneer, Wilhelm Kress, developed the stick control for aircraft but did not apply for a patent. It was later awarded to the French aviator, Robert Esnault-Pelterie, who applied for it in 1907.

Kress, who had developed a hang-glider in 1877, was one of several pioneers who could lay claim to having made a breakthrough in flying machines.

PARISIAN UNDERGROUND

The Metropolitan, or Metro, underground system, opened in Paris on July 19. 'Line 1', as it was called, ran from Porte de Vincennes to Porte Maillot as part of a planned six line network. Construction of an underground system in New York City also began this year.

DEATHS

March 6 – German motor car designer and builder, Gottlieb Daimler.
April 30 – US railway engineer, Casey Jones.

Toys

GERMAN MASS APPEAL

The Edwardian child's toys and games were still largely made in Germany, as had been the case for their Victorian predecessors. The UK led in the production of wax dolls, whilst the French made the most luxurious dolls.

No other country could compete with German toy production for sheer value for money. The most popular toys continued to be dolls, clockwork toys, boats, puzzles, trains, dolls' houses, toy animals and rocking horses.

TOY TRAIN PIONEER

In 1900, 22-year-old, Joshua Lionel Cowen, from Manhattan, created a battery-powered train engine as an 'animated advertisement' for products in a shop's display window.

To his surprise, customers were more interested in purchasing this than the merchandise in the display. The shop owner ordered six more trains from him to sell. That same year, Cowen founded the Lionel Manufacturing Co., which was to become one of the world's biggest manufacturer's of toy trains. The company later made some of the first electric trains.

Cowen had a flair for invention at an early age. At that time, trains were either pushed along the floor or powered by steam engines fired by burning alcohol – not particularly suitable for children!

When he was seven, Cowen built his first toy train – attaching a small steam engine to a wooden locomotive he had carved. The engine exploded, damaging his parents' kitchen.

In 1899, he received his first patent for a device that ignited a photographer's flash. It was followed by a contract from the US Navy to produce mine fuses that netted him $12,000.

But his love of trains remained with him and it continued to delight generations of children (and their fathers) after him.

Sport

OLYMPICS OVERSHADOWED

The second modern Olympic Games, which were held in Paris, were overshadowed by the Exposition Universalle (Paris Exhibition).

With all the city's attention focussed on the grand Exhibition, the Olympics were viewed as a sideshow. In fact, it was rarely referred to as 'Olympic'. Instead it was variously called the International Championships, Paris Championships and even 'Grand Prix' of the Paris Exposition.

There was no opening or closing ceremony, and most of the winners did not receive medals, but were given cups or trophies. The Games were given such a low profile that many athletes died without ever knowing that they had participated in the Olympics!

The Games, which were won by the US, were notable for allowing women to compete for the first time. Britain's Charlotte Cooper became the first female Olympic champion when she won the tennis singles.

QUEENSBERRY RULES

Sporting patron, the Marquess of Queensberry, father of the modern rules of boxing, died on January 31.

A keen, all-round sportsman, he was one of the founders of the Amateur Athletic Club in 1866, which became the Amateur Athletic Association. The following year, the Club published a set of 12 rules for conducting boxing matches. Although drawn up by John Graham Chambers, they appeared under Queensberry's sponsorship and became known as the 'Marquess of Queensberry Rules'.

'DAVIS CUP' IS BORN

US tennis player, Dwight F. Davis, created a new tennis tournament between the US and Great Britain, which was to become the Davis Cup.

At the US Tennis Championships in 1898, Davis was the runner-up for the men's singles title and, together with Holcombe Ward, dominated the men's double event, winning at the Championships for three years in a row from 1899 to 1901.

In 1900 Davis, along with three other players, developed the structure for a new tournament known as the International Lawn Tennis Challenge. He was a member of the US team that won the first two competitions in 1900 and 1902, and was also the captain of the 1900 team. It was renamed the Davis Cup, after he died in 1945.

KNOCK-OUT BLOW

Jim Jeffries of the US, had an epic battle with James J. Corbett to retain his world heavyweight boxing title.

Jeffries had become a champion by defeating British-born Bob Fitzsimmons the previous year, but it looked like his title was slipping away after 22 rounds with former champion, Corbett, in New York.

Corbett had boxed masterfully and looked set to regain the title when a left hook to the jaw knocked him out.

The Home

MIDDLE AND UPPER CLASSES

Homes in the latter part of the Nineteenth Century were greatly influenced in style by William Morris and the Arts and Crafts movement. Heavy curtains, dark ornate wallpaper and imposing handmade furniture jostled for space with a plethora of ornaments, paintings and plants, giving the living space an elegant but cluttered appearance.

Art Noveau décor began to be introduced around 1900, bringing furniture with ornate scrolls, flower designs, weaving vines and leaves.

Flushing toilets and inside bathrooms were also introduced, and water was brought into kitchens by pumps.

The well-to-do Victorian lady, like her Edwardian counterpart, rarely lifted a finger in her own house: cooks and maids were commonplace, even for the middle classes. For the bigger, wealthier houses, a staff of 20 was not unusual. The duty of a good wife and mother was to organise the household and make sure it ran smoothly.

Mealtimes in these houses were a rigid, formal affair, and punctuality was demanded, so as not to upset the routine of the servants. For them, the day began early, with breakfast preparations and heating of water for the household ablutions starting at 6 am. Work then continued until the last dishes were washed at night.

LOWER CLASSES

Homes for the poorer classes differed greatly between town and country. The many families who had moved towards towns and cities during the Victorian era led to cramped conditions. Large families housed in one or two rooms could afford only the bare minimum of furniture, with a bed or two, some chairs and a stove for heat and cooking. The lack of available water meant these homes were impossible to keep clean and they soon degenerated into slums.

For those who still had jobs in the country, life was a little brighter. As well as the advantage of wide open space and clean air, farmers often allowed their workers a small plot of land to grow fresh fruit and vegetables, so good food was in plentiful supply. Milk from the local dairy farmer was cheap, and many cottagers kept chickens for eggs and meat or bred rabbits for the pot. Bread was baked at home, and the country families had a healthy diet of vegetable stews, soup and the occasional piece of bacon or chicken.

The Changing Role of Women

Although women still had few rights at the turn of the century, some Victorian trailblazers had fought for the right to a university education and many had begun to establish careers outside of traditional factory work and domestic service.

Girton college, the first university college for women, was set up in 1870 but was not recognised by the authorities. Ten years later, Newnham college opened at Cambridge university but by the turn of the century it was still rare for women to go on to further education and they were not allowed to take degrees.

Without official qualifications, women struggled to enter the professions. By 1900, there were 200 female doctors in the country, but women were not permitted to be accountants, barristers, bankers or diplomats.

Marital laws had changed during the period, in favour of wives, with two significant acts. The first, passed in 1870, granted limited rights to hold on to property after marriage and to retain up to £200 of their own wages, if they worked. In 1883, a revised act allowed women to acquire and retain any property and monies that could be deemed separate from their husband's effects. For the first time, they were granted the same legal protection as men if they needed to defend the right to property.

SUFFRAGETTES

The National Union of Women's Suffrage had been founded by Millicent Fawcett in 1897, in a bid to gain voting rights for women, but the peaceful protests and logical argument of the early day 'suffragettes' had garnered little support as yet. The fight was to start in earnest two years later, when Emmeline Pankhurst and her daughters founded rival group the 'Women's Social and Political Union'.

Science

THE BROWNIE CAMERA

The arrival of the cheap and cheerful Kodak Brownie camera was a sensation. Designed and marketed with children in mind, it made photography accessible to the masses.

It consisted of a basic cardboard box camera with a simple lens and controls. It was intended to be a camera that anyone could afford and use.

Low in material cost and high in production, it cost just one dollar to buy and was an instant success. Aggressive marketing saw the camera appear in many trade magazines and an international sales network ensured its popularity around the world.

The camera was invented by Frank Brownell, a subcontractor of Eastman Kodak, who named it after the popular cartoon characters of the time, the *Brownies*, created by children's author and illustrator, Palmer Cox.

QUANTUM THEORY

Professor Max Planck, of Berlin University, made the breakthrough discovery that energy was not continuous but came in small units and

The technologically advanced Paris Expo saw many developments, including the escalator and an engine run on peanut oil. (Image courtesy of the Estate of Stanley Shoop).

that the movement of the elementary particles was random. He called these units 'quanta' and so his proposal was named the 'Quantum Theory'.

DREAMS UNLOCKED

Austrian psychiatrist and neurologist, Sigmund Freud, published *The Interpretation of Dreams.*

Freud argued that dreams were not just ramblings, but forms of wish fulfilment, expressing the frustrations and resentments of our waking hours. Freud suggested that some of our wishes may be socially un-acceptable and so were suppressed by day.

He put forward a psychological technique to interpret dreams and said of his work. 'Insight such as this falls to one's lot but once in a lifetime.'

GAMMA-RAYS

French chemist and physicist, Paul Villard, discovered gamma rays whilst studying uranium decay.

He recognised them as being different from x rays because the gamma rays had a much greater penetrating depth.

Gamma rays were emitted from radioactive substances and were not affected by electric or magnetic fields.

THE EXPOSITION UNIVERSALLE

The first working escalator, patented a year earlier, was unveiled at the 'Exposition Universalle' (Paris Expedition) in 1900. Manufactured by the Otis Elevator Company, it was installed in a Philadelphia office building the following year.

Rudolf Diesel, who invented the diesel engine in 1892, also caused a stir when he exhibited his engine running on peanut oil.

Chapter Two

1901

Introduction

QUEEN VICTORIA'S demise, in January 1901, ushered in the bright, optimistic Edwardian era. The decade over which Victoria's son, Edward VII, was to preside saw massive changes which would affect every aspect of daily life.

Queen Victoria, seen here with her great-grandchildren, the children of the Duke and Duchess of Cornwall and York, had reigned over Britain for the lifetime of many of her subjects, her death after almost 64 years on the throne promised many changes.

Politics

SALISBURY TAKES FIRM STAND AGAINST IRISH

The PM, Lord Salisbury, firmly ruled out self-government for Ireland. In an uncompromising statement, he said that Britain's military power could be undermined if Home Rule were ever conceded.

Speaking to the Non-Conformist Association, he warned how a free and hostile Ireland might have hindered the Government's war effort in South Africa.

He said, 'If it defies the might of England it defies one of the most formidable enemies it could possibly encounter.'

CHURCHILL ENTERS THE HOUSE

Winston Churchill, the 26-year-old Conservative Member for Oldham, took his seat in the House of Commons.

AUSTRALIAN INDEPENDENCE

On January 1, the Commonwealth of Australia came into being. The six colonies that made up Australia were federated under an act of the British Parliament on January 1, and on May 9, Australia opened its first parliament in Melbourne.

US PRESIDENT ASSASSINATED

The world was shocked when US President William McKinley was assassinated by a gunman. Anarchist Leon Czolgosz shot him on September 6 at the Pan-American Exposition in Buffalo, New York, where he died eight days later.

Czolgosz, 28, fired at the President after he waited in line with other members of the public for a meet and greet.

In his right hand, Czolgosz held a 32 caliber revolver, which he had covered by wrapping a handkerchief around the gun and his hand. The President assumed he had injured his hand, but Czolgosz then fired two shots. One of the bullets missed – some say it bounced off a button – but the other entered through his abdomen, tearing through his internal organs.

As he sagged, bleeding to the floor, the President told those around him, 'Be careful how you tell my wife.'

William McKinley was the third President of the United States to be assassinated. Kennedy would be the fourth.

Czolgosz was quickly apprehended by guards and the President was rushed to hospital. For several days, the President seemed to be getting better, and the nation held its breath. But an infection set in and he died on September 14 of gangrene. That afternoon, Vice President Theodore Roosevelt was sworn in as the 26th President of the United States.

In his written confession, Czolgosz stated, 'I killed President McKinley because I've done my duty. I didn't believe one man should have so much service and another man should have none.'

He was brought to trial on September 23, quickly found guilty, and on October 29, 1901, Czolgosz was electrocuted.

Royalty

END OF AN ERA

Queen Victoria died at her seaside home, Osborne, on the Isle of Wight, aged 81, on January 22. Many of her children and grandchildren were at

Britain mourned for her (then) longest reigning monarch.

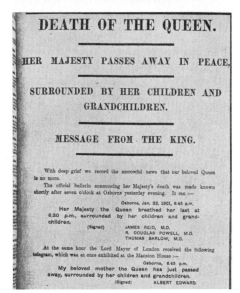

* MESSAGE FROM HIS MAJESTY THE KING TO THE ARMY.

Osborne.
25th January, 1901.

On my accession to the Throne of my Ancestors I am desirous of thanking the Army for the splendid services which it has rendered to my beloved Mother The Queen during Her Glorious Reign of upwards of 63 years.

Her Majesty invariably evinced the warmest interest in Her Troops, especially when on active service, both as a Sovereign and as the Head of Her Army, and She was proud of the fact of being a Soldier's Daughter.

To secure your best interests will be one of the dearest objects of my heart, and I know I can count upon that loyal devotion which you ever evinced towards your late Sovereign.

EDWARD R.I.

+ ORDERS FOR MOURNING FOR THE ARMY OF HER LATE MAJESTY QUEEN VICTORIA, TO BE WORN UNTIL 24TH JULY, 1901.

1. His Majesty the King commands that officers of the Army shall wear mourning with their uniforms on the present melancholy occasion, as follows :—
Officers are to wear black crape on the left arm of the uniform and of the greatcoat.

2. The drums are to be covered with black, and black crape is to be hung from the top of the Colour staff of Infantry, and from the Standard staff and trumpets of Cavalry, until after the funeral of Her late Majesty.

DEATH OF THE QUEEN.

HER MAJESTY PASSES AWAY IN PEACE,

SURROUNDED BY HER CHILDREN AND GRANDCHILDREN.

MESSAGE FROM THE KING.

With deep grief we record the sorrowful news that our beloved Queen is no more.

The official bulletin announcing her Majesty's death was made known shortly after seven o'clock at Osborne yesterday evening. It ran :—

Osborne, Jan. 22, 1901, 6.45 p.m.
Her Majesty the Queen breathed her last at 6.30 p.m., surrounded by her children and grandchildren.

(Signed) JAMES REID, M.D.
R. DOUGLAS POWELL, M.D.
THOMAS BARLOW, M.D.

At the same hour the Lord Mayor of London received the following telegram, which was at once exhibited at the Mansion House :—

Osborne, 6.45 p.m.
My beloved mother the Queen has just passed away, surrounded by her children and grandchildren.
(Signed) ALBERT EDWARD.

Announcing his own accession, Edward VII, announced the orders for mourning to his army.

The new king, Edward VII, sent a telegram to the Lord Mayor of London announcing the death of his mother, Queen Victoria, seen here on the front page of *The Daily Mail*.

her bedside. She had reigned for 63 years – longer than any other British sovereign – during which time the mighty British Empire stretched around the globe.

The Queen and her husband, Prince Albert, had nine children, several of whom married into other royal families, earning her the title of 'Grandmother of Europe'.

She never got over the death from typhoid of her husband, in 1861, and became reclusive, wearing black mourning clothes for 40 years.

During her reign, she saw ten Prime Ministers come and go and her worldly experience was treated with great respect.

On her death, her eldest son, Edward VII, acceded to the throne at the age of 59. Edward, who was formally known as The Prince of Wales, had a playboy reputation with many mistresses, including actresses Sarah Bernhardt and Lillie Langtry. Despite his parents concerns that he was too frivolous to be monarch, he rose to the occasion and immediately revived the full pomp and pageantry of the 'State Opening of Parliament' – a ceremony which Victoria had allowed to lapse.

Crowds lined the streets of London as the new monarch and his wife, Queen Alexandra, drove in full state splendour from Buckingham Palace to Westminster, to open the first parliament of his reign.

Queen Victoria's funeral was held at St George's Chapel, in the precincts of Windsor Castle. After lying in state for two days, her body was interred in the Frogmore Royal Mausoleum at Windsor Home Park, beside her beloved husband.

BIRTH

Princess Alice, Duchess of Gloucester, was born on Christmas Day. The wife of Prince Henry, Duke of Gloucester, the third son of George V and Queen Mary, she reached the ripe old age of 102, when she died in October 2004.

Historical Events

CHINA HIT BY BOXER REBELLION

China paid dearly for the Boxer uprising, which officially ended on September 7, when the country signed a peace protocol drawn up by a dozen foreign powers.

The crippling conditions imposed on China included China agreeing to pay war reparations of £65m, and to permit the stationing of troops from the allied nations both in Peking and in the main ports. Various commercial agreements were made which were favourable to the victorious countries and many high-ranking officials linked to the hostilities were ordered to be executed.

The Imperial Government's humiliating failure to defend China against the foreign powers contributed to the growth of nationalist resentment.

BOER WAR RUMBLES ON

Field Marshall Lord Roberts had assumed that the war would end with the capture of the Boer capitals and the dispersal of the main Boer armies. But he reckoned without a new phase of guerilla warfare.

With the arrival of extra troops, the British army, now under the command of Lord Kitchener, boasted around 250,000 men. But the Boers used guerrilla tactics to great success.

The vast distances of the Republics allowed the Boer commandos considerable freedom to move about and made it impossible for British troops to control the territory effectively. As soon as they left a town or district, British control of that area went with them.

The commandos had the advantage of knowing the districts and the terrain, and their knowledge of farming meant they could live off the land. They garnered local support with simple orders to act against the British whenever possible.

Damaging blows continued to be dealt at slow-moving British columns by the commandos who attacked quickly and withdrew before reinforcements could arrive. Although Boer morale began to fall as British might gradually wore them down.

STUDENT RIOTS IN RUSSIA

Russian students, leading the political opposition to the Tsarist Government, held a mass demonstration in St Petersburg. It followed the Government's new powers to curb the activities of student organisations. The demonstrators handed out leaflets calling for freedom and the downfall of the Tsar, before two regiments of Cossacks were called in to break them up. Over 800 were arrested.

Social Change

THE NEW COMMUTER

Improved transport links in the first decade of the Twentieth Century had two major effects on social change. Firstly, more everyday goods began to be imported which meant less agricultural work was available. Secondly, it was now possible to live in the outskirts of a town or city and travel in to the centre for work. The first commuters were born.

Areas near cities, such as Dulwich in south-east London and Saltaire near Leeds, saw more and more houses being built to cope with the growth of the middle-class commuter. In 1901, only nine and a half per cent of the population worked on the land, compared with twenty-three and a half per cent 50 years earlier. As more goods were imported, traditional crafts such as lace making, basket weaving and cabinet making began to die out.

FACTORY WORK

Factories still thrived and provided work for many, but the industrial revolution meant there were less jobs. The 1901 census, for example, showed a three-point-one per cent decline in the cotton industry, which had been one of the major employers of the industrial age.

Work in factories was still long and hard, but conditions were improving. Towards the end of the Nineteenth Century, the Victorians had passed several factory acts banning the employment of children under 11 and limiting the hours of eleven to 14-year-olds and women. The 1901 'Factories Act' consolidated several health and safety regulations, covering maternity arrangements, employment of children, wages, night work and fire escapes. Nonetheless, every month, more than 300 people were killed and between 8,000 and 10,000 injured as a result of industrial accidents.

RICH-POOR DIVIDE

Domestic service was still a major form of employment, as wages were low and even the middle classes could afford a maid. They generally lived with the family and had a sparse bedroom in the attic. The 1901 census recorded 1,690,686 women 'in service'.

The biggest growth sector in employment noted in the 1901 census was the white collar workers. In ten years, the number of men in the telegraph and telephone services grew by 53 per cent; in local government by 37 per cent; and as merchants, agents and buyers by 37 per cent.

Britain was seen as a prosperous nation. The average wage, per head, had risen from £34.90 in 1874 to £42.70 in 1900. But the rich-poor divide was enormous, with half the nation's income going to one-ninth of its population.

Fashion

ROYAL FASHION SETTER

The death of Victoria ushered in a subtle change in female fashion and the birth of the Edwardian Lady. Even as the Princess of Wales, Alexandra had been considered a trendsetter, and she was elevated to the level of fashion icon on her husband's accession to the throne.

Queen Alexandra wore her hair piled high on her head, a distinctive multi-stranded pearl choker and beautiful couture dresses which inspired many a society lady. She was also strong-willed, saying of her Coronation dress, 'I know better than all the milliners and antiquaries. I shall wear exactly what I like and so will all my ladies. Basta!'

But Alexandra's style didn't come cheap. She chose London fashion houses, such as Redfern, for patriotic reasons, but occasionally allowed herself a shopping trip in Paris, where she favoured Doucet, Fromont and the English-born Charles Worth. For the increasing numbers of middle class in society, the price tag of these dresses was too high and dressmakers all over the country were employed to come up with passable copies.

Even the elaborate hairstyles modelled by the Queen required some wealth, as they were almost impossible to recreate without a lady's maid. She would have her hair wound around pads, charmingly dubbed 'rats', and secured with pins and combs.

The hairstyle worked well with that trademark of Edwardian style – the picture hat. The creations were decorated with huge ostrich or osprey feathers and floral arrangements, and could cost as much as 50 guineas (equivalent to £3,700 today).

LIGHTER AND MORE FEMININE

One of the major changes of the period was in the materials used in dresses. The stiff satins, tweed and damask of the Victorian period made way for lighter choices, such as chiffon, lace and crêpe de Chine, leading to a frothier, more feminine style.

However, the basic silhouette among the more affluent ladies was to remain unchanged from the 'S' Line until 1908 and the corset was still very much in evidence.

In fact, even the servants, who had neither the time nor the money for fashion, were expected to wear corsets, which often made their domestic work much harder. Bending down to scrub floors must have been a terrible strain in such rigid undergarments.

Maids were generally given three sets of working clothes – a print dress for the dirty work, a black dress and white cap for serving, and another outfit for time off and church on Sundays. These they paid for out of their own wages.

As the upper echelons of society judged their contemporaries on wardrobe, the poorer members had little need for fashion. Even the dressmakers, slaving over the gowns for middle class ladies, could only dream of owning a similar dress themselves, earning between 2s6d and 3s6d a day by the end of the decade.

Entertainment

FILM

It was only five years since the first film had been shown by the Lumiere Brothers in the Regent Street Polytechnic in London, and cinema was in its infancy. The earlier films had depicted simple events such as a train arriving at a station, and had been jerky, with black spots appearing frequently.

Local entrepreneurs, such as Sagar Mitchell and James Kenyon (who were based in Blackburn at the turn of the century), began to document everyday life by filming groups of workers leaving their factory or workplace. These could always guarantee a local audience of people anxious to see themselves or their friends in 'moving pictures'.

By 1901, films often depicted news events, such as the funeral of Queen Victoria, and were even being used as propaganda. One film called *The Dispatch Rider,* showed an English soldier giving a Boer a drink and then being shot in the back. The action was completely faked.

Other popular movies included drama and comedy, including the popular French film *The Man with the Rubber Head,* which used camera trickery for a visual gag. A chemist used bellows and a rubber tube to inflate his own head and then deflated it. When his assistant attempted the same experiment he went too far and his head exploded.

With film still at a premium ,the features were always very short, with

100 feet of film amounting to just 100 seconds. Cinemas themselves had not yet been erected, so the majority of 'pictures' were seen in empty shops, furnished with folding seats. The novelty was still huge and the public flocked to pay their penny and see their first flick.

One event that was to shape the future of cinema was the birth of Walt Disney. The pioneering artist was born on December 5, and would go on to achieve a revolution in animated films, receiving forty-eight Oscar nominations and winning twenty-two Oscars.

BIRTHS

February 1– Clark Gable, actor.
February 9 – Brian Donlevy, actor.
February 10 – Stella Adler,actress and teacher.
February 25 – Zeppo Marx, actor and comedian.
May 7 – Gary Cooper, actor.
May 21– Sam Jaffe, director and producer.
June 29 – Nelson Eddy, actor.
August 4 – Louis Armstrong, actor and musician.
December 5 – Walt Disney, animator.
December 27 – Marlene Dietrich, actress.

THEATRE AND MUSIC HALLS

In December 1901, the Hackney Empire opened its doors to music hall fans who flocked in their hundreds. Vaudeville theatre had been considered too crude for ladies during the Victorian era but, by the turn of the century, performers such as Marie Lloyd, Vesta Tilley and George Robey played to packed houses of both sexes in London and towns throughout the UK.

This cheap and convenient form

Ellen Terry ruled the West End stage

of theatre consisted of a variety of acts, and therefore people could come and go during performances and, more importantly for many, could smoke in the theatre – a luxury not allowed in the upmarket venues.

For the more affluent members of society, the West End provided glimpses of such great actors as Henry Irving, Samuel Phelps and Ellen Terry.

STANISLAVSKY

In 1901, Constantin Stanislavsky was to change the face of theatre forever. The Russian actor, director and founder of the Moscow Art Theatre, formulated the revolutionary *Stanislavsky Method*, which replaced melo-drama with realism. His teachings required actors to absorb themselves into the character and react on stage as they would in real life. New York acting coach Lee Strasberg later popularised 'Method acting' in the 1940s and 50s. Many of today's actors, including Dustin Hoffman, Jack Nicholson and Al Pacino, were schooled in 'The Method'.

Literature

1901 saw the first Nobel prizes awarded, five years after the death of Alfred Nobel. The first prize for literature, awarded to French author Sully Prudhomme (pen name of René François Armand Prudhomme) turned out to be a controversial one. Many scholars were outraged that Russian writer Leo Tolstoy was not chosen. In October, Mark Twain, American author of *The Adventures of Tom Sawyer* and *The Prince and the Pauper,* received an honorary doctorate from Yale University.

Rudyard Kipling's novel *Kim*, which centred on the orphaned son of an Irish soldier who was growing up as a vagabond in Lahore, was published. It was immediately hailed as his masterpiece.

Other literary works published included Emile Zola's *Travail*, Miles Franklin's *My Brilliant Career* and H.G.Wells' futuristic novel *The First Men in the Moon*.

Civil rights campaigner Booker T. Washington published *Up from Slavery*, an autobiography charting his journey from a childhood in slavery to an education at Hampton University. The same year, he was awarded an honorary doctorate from Dartmouth College in New Hampshire.

A historical novel called *The Crisis* was published in America, written by Winston Churchill. This was not, however, the future Prime Minister of Britain but a distant American cousin!

BIRTHS:

April 10 – Anna Kavan, British novelist.
July 19 – Dame Barbara Cartland, romantic novelist.
January 6 – Tomas Gudmundsson, Icelandic poet.

DEATHS:

June 9 – Sir Walter Bessant, novelist and historian.
July 7 – Johanna Spyri, Swiss author and creator of *Heidi*.

Architecture

Many homes had glass conservatories or glass-roofed lobbies, serving as sun-traps. White painted walls replaced the austere dark colours favoured before, and homes became light and airy.

In public buildings, the architecture began to hark back to the eighteenth century style of Sir Christopher Wren and the Edwardian Baroque movement was born.

Typically, the buildings would feature rusticated basements, round arches and Ionic columns, as well as the domes made famous by Wren

H. G. Wells' futuristic novel, *The First Men in the Moon* was published in instalments in *The Strand Magazine*.

himself. Mansard roofs, with steep lower walls and a much flatter top, were favoured and dormer windows were common. Many buildings constructed in the Edwardian period, between 1901 and 1910, borrowed so faithfully from Wren inspiration that they were dubbed 'Wrenaissance'.

Westminster Central Hall and The Central Criminal Court (Old Bailey) are prime examples of Edwardian Baroque buildings, as is Nottingham Railway Station, a magnificent red brick and terracotta construction, which cost £1 million to build and was designed in 1901.

CARNEGIE LIBRARIES

Having sold his share in his Carnegie Steel Co, Scots-born entrepreneur Andrew Carnegie became the richest man in the world. He immediately vowed to put his money to a worthy cause. On March 12, 1901, he wrote to the authorities in New York and offered to fund the building of branch libraries in the city. Two months later, he wrote to the City of Glasgow officials with a similar offer.

This generous gift led to 12 libraries being built in the city, seven of which were designed by architect James Rhind. Of these, five are in the Edwardian Baroque style which, at that time, was rare in Scotland. Rhind's striking plans created landmark buildings in rundown areas with flamboyant use of columns, domes and statues.

The Carnegie programme actually began in 1879 when Carnegie donated £5000 to build a library in his hometown of Dunfermline, Scotland. This continued benevolence would eventually result in 1,946 new libraries in the United States, 660 in Britain and Ireland and 156 in Canada.

FRANK LLOYD WRIGHT

American architect Frank Lloyd Wright made history by designing his first Prairie home. The Ward W. Willits house, in Highland Park, Illinois, is the earliest example of the sprawling homes that would become synonymous with the notorious designer. Built around a wood frame, it has a symmetrical façade and is planned in a cruciform shape, with four wings spreading out from a central chimney core.

PHILADELPHIA CITY HALL

Completed in 1901, the city's government building stands at 167 metres (548 ft) and, until 1908, was the tallest habitable building in the world.

Designed by Scottish architect John McArthur Jr., it took 30 years to complete and cost $24 million (£12 million).

Originally designed to be the world's tallest building, it was surpassed during that time by the Washington Monument and the Eiffel Tower. The limestone, granite and marble structure boasts walls that are 22 feet thick and it is topped by an 11.3 m (37 ft), 27-ton bronze figure of city founder William Penn, the tallest rooftop statue in the world.

Art

VINCENT VAN GOGH

On March 17, 11 years after his suicide, an exhibition of the works of Vincent van Gogh opened at the Galeries Bernheim-Jeune in Paris. The exhibition, put together by French art critic Julien LeClercq, contained 71 paintings borrowed from art collectors and dealers. Amongst them were two versions of the now famous *Sunflowers*, one of which some experts have since suggested may be a fake.

The event brought van Gogh to the attention of German dealer Paul Cassirer who then arranged a similar showing in Berlin. With the assistance of van Gogh's sister-in-law Johanna van Gogh-Bonger, Cassirer created a market and then set about controlling prices, paving the way for the astronomical price tags of today.

In 1990, van Gogh's *Portrait of Dr Gachet* sold at Christie's, New York, for $129.7 million (£65 million).

PABLO PICASSO

The shock death of a close friend in 1901 led to Pablo Picasso's famous 'blue period'. Picasso and his fellow painter Carlos Casagemas were living in Paris when the latter, spurned by the woman he loved, shot himself in a café. The event had a profound effect on Picasso who would revisit it in his art for years to come. His *Death of Casagemas* was his first 'blue painting'. 'I began to paint in blue, when I realized that Casagemas had died,' he later wrote. *Le Noces de Pierrette*, from this period, was sold at auction in 1989 for $51.7 million (£26 million).

TOULOUSE-LAUTREC

September 9 saw the untimely death of French artist Henri de Toulouse-Lautrec. Born into an aristocratic family in the South of France, Henri's growth was stunted when he broke both his legs as a child. As an adult, he moved to Paris where he was inspired by the nightlife of Montmatre and the showgirls and prostitutes he met there.

A heavy drinker, Toulouse-Lautrec had a breakdown in 1899 and was confined to a clinic. In 1901, he suffered a stroke and was moved to his mother's castle home on August 20 where he died, three weeks later, at the age of 36.

In November 2005, *La Blanchisseuse*, a portrait of washer women, was sold for $22.4 million (£11.2 million), a world record for the artist.

Travel and Transport

COMFORTABLE TRAINS

At the turn of the century, transport was the fastest evolving aspect of everyday life. Trains, now a familiar feature for 50 years, were still a cheap and popular means of travelling long distances, and carried around 1.2 million passengers a year at a price of ½p a mile. Carriages were more comfortable than in the early days, with heating and restaurant cars, and could travel up to 70 mph.

TRAMS AND CARS INCREASINGLY POPULAR

In cities, towns and villages, horse-drawn carriages still dominated the streets, but they were slowly being usurped by electric trams and the growing popularity of the motor car. Trams had previously been horse-drawn, powered by steam or pulled by cables, but the use of electricity

The King Edward VII train was built in 1901and was used to transport the royal family.

Electric trams were becoming increasingly widespread and were popular in coastal resorts, such as Llandudno and Ramsgate, as well as London.

was spread through the northern towns in the late 1890s and, in 1901, was adopted in London.

Another affordable way to travel was the omnibus. At the beginning of 1901, services in London were still horse-drawn, but in September *The Times* announced 'a service of motor cars . . . to carry passengers, at omnibus fares, between Piccadilly Circus and Putney'. The ten horse-power wagonettes carried up to eight people.

The earliest motor cars had been available in Britain from 1895, but many people were hostile to their introduction. The law allowed them to go at 4 mph, but they had to be preceded by a man waving a red flag. By 1901, the flag bearer was gone and the speed limit had been raised to a whopping 14 mph! Even so, the price of a 'horseless carriage' was so prohibitive that they were largely playthings for the rich and adventurous.

Rudyard Kipling, who bought his first car in 1897, described an outing as a series of 'agonies, shames, delays, rages, chills, parboilings, road-walkings, water-drawings, burns and starvations'.

Things were moving faster overseas, with France, Germany and the US particularly taken with the new cars. The first car manufacturers were the French companies Panhard & Levassor (est. 1889) and Peugeot (est. 1891), who cornered the UK market, but the first mass-produced car was the 'curved dash oldsmobile', built by American manufacturer Ransom Eli Olds. In 1901, the year of its introduction, 425 were sold in the US and in the same year, New York State became the first to require licence plates.

Cycling had enjoyed a huge increase in popularity in the 1890s, due to the introduction of the safety cycle, which made riding easier for ladies. It continued to be a popular way to get around in 1901, with the census recording that 50,000 workers were involved in the manufacture of bicycles.

Toys

The social divide between rich and poor was as marked in childhood as in adulthood for Edwardian children. While upper class nurseries boasted rocking horses, doll's houses and train sets, poorer children usually made do with a whip and top, a skipping rope or hoop and stick.

Many of the most common toys and games were imported, the majority from Germany. UK-produced wax dolls were on the market, as were the expensive French equivalents, but German toys represented the best value for money, so that even the less affluent families could afford the occasional toy for their children.

Mechanical toys were still a rarity, but clockwork animals and 'humming tin spinning-tops' were popular, as were the clockwork trains and, for the more wealthy, steam-powered engines.

In 1901, train engineer Frank Hornby patented his 'Mechanics Made Easy' set. In a bid to teach his two sons the basics of engineering, Hornby came up with a toy consisting of metal strips and plates with nuts and bolts to fasten them together. The name of these successful sets was changed to Meccano in 1907 and the Meccano Company was set up in 1908.

Sport

Improved transport at the beginning of the Twentieth Century meant that weekend parties became more frequent and the popularity of hunting and fishing increased. Hunting was one of the few sports that women participated in and became so popular that foxes were imported from Europe to meet demand!

For the common man, however, football was the great spectator sport.

THE ' CROUCH SMASH."
Another sensational coup invented by the Ping-Pong champion.
His opponent generally finds that this is practically unplayable.

Table tennis was becoming highly popular and had its first championships in December. They were won by a 13-year-old.

In April 1901, Hotspur FC (later renamed Tottenham Hotspur) won the FA cup after beating Sheffield United by 3–1, in a replay at Burden Park in Bolton. The first game, which resulted in a 2–2 draw at Crystal Palace, saw the first six-figure attendance for a football match with 114, 815 spectators.

The occasion was also notable in that it sparked the first 'video replay'. Both matches were screened on the Monday after the game, to the triumphant strains of the Tottenham Brass band, and the playback proved conclusively that the referee should not have awarded Sheffield their second goal in the first match.

There was another controversy in January 1901, when the Football Association called for a stoppage on all football matches on Saturday after Queen Victoria's death. The Southern League, which consisted of six clubs including West Ham, Millwall and Southampton, objected on the grounds that it infringed a player's right to earn a living. Four of their fixtures went ahead.

Elsewhere, the new game of table tennis was gaining popularity and had its first championships in December. The game, dubbed ding-dong or ping-pong, was not popular with one reporter from *The Times*, especially when the championship was won by a 13-year-old. He wrote, 'One is inclined to think that a game at which a child can compete on equal terms with grown men cannot make much of a claim to be considered anything but an occupation for the idlest, slackest hours.'

BIRTHS

January 20 – Cecil Griffiths, British athlete.
January 21 – Ricardo Zamora, Spanish football player.
August 26 – Frankie Genaro, US boxer.
December 14 – Henri Cochet, French tennis player.

DEATHS

October 26 – Alfred Tysoe, British athlete and Olympic gold medallist.

The Home

The homes of the Edwardian era differed greatly depending on class. In his study of York in 1901, Seebohm Rowntree concluded that 28 per cent of the population of the city was living in poverty. The homes of the very poorest, he wrote, 'hidden away in dark and narrow streets are indeed miserable dwellings'. His description of one home read 'House no.4. Two rooms, seven inmates. Walls, ceiling and furniture filthy. Dirty flock bedding in living room placed on a box and two chairs. Children pale, starved-looking and only half-clothed.'

As more middle class homes began to be built, there were major changes in design. The kitchen, which had traditionally been in the basement, moved up to the ground floor to become lighter and more airy. White walls became fashionable and the dark, cluttered, Victorian rooms gave way to light and space. Fitted bathrooms were becoming popular, meaning less carrying of water, and kitchen ranges were slowly being replaced with gas stoves, whilst oil lamps made way for gas lamps or even electricity. Gardens, which had been full of shrubs, burst with colourful flower beds which reflected the optimism of the new reign.

For both middle and upper class homes, the kitchen was still the domain of the servants and, with few labour saving devices available, everything was done by hand. Cleaning, cooking and laundry were long-winded and arduous tasks, and in the larger houses, a team of domestic staff would be overseen by a housekeeper and a butler.

In the large country homes of the more affluent classes, a team of gardeners and grooms was also necessary to tend to the grounds and the horses. As the motor car grew in popularity, however, grooms and coachmen began to be replaced with chauffeurs, who were also expected to be mechanics.

The Changing Role of Women

Victorian values dictated that the woman's place was in the home; 'respectable' wives wouldn't dream of working. Yet the 1901 census shows that nearly a third of women were in paid employment and in a wide variety of jobs. Nearly 80 per cent were either in domestic service or manufacturing, but other occupations listed include lawyers' clerks, physicians, dentists or dental assistants, teachers, authors, journalists and shorthand writers.

With no social benefit available, most women worked as an economic necessity, whether it be because they were single, widowed or in a low income family. A small minority, however, worked out of choice and were becoming increasingly ambitious.

In Macclesfield infirmary, in Ceshire, the appointment of a female doctor caused uproar. Her male colleagues walked out and she was forced to resign. A letter to *The Times* the same year argued that giving young ladies jobs in the city was 'a gigantic mistake' and that domestic work was better suited to their training as a future wife.

Science

Italian inventor Guglielmo Marconi demonstrated that his wireless signals were not affected by the curvature of the earth when he transmitted a signal across the Atlantic between Cornwall and St. John's, New-foundland, a distance of 21,000 miles.

German surgeon Eugen Hollander carried out the first recorded face lift at the behest of a Polish baroness. The lady came up with the idea that if the skin in front of her ears was removed, the skin on her lower face would be tightened. She sketched her plan and Hollander obliged, creating a procedure that would become the foundation of a multi-million dollar beauty industry.

British engineer Hubert Cecil Booth, was granted a patent for a vacuum cleaner on August 30. As yet, it was unlikely to benefit the average house-wife. This vacuum was a huge, horse-drawn, petrol-driven machine which had to be parked outside a building, while long hoses were fed through the window! At the same time, two American inventors were coming up with similar devices. Corinne Dufour's cleaner sucked dust into a wet sponge, while David E. Kenney's had to be housed in a cellar with a series of tubes leading to each room in the house.

THE NOBEL PRIZE IS BORN

On December 10, five years after the death of Swedish chemist Alfred Nobel, the first awards were given out in his name. The Nobel Prize for outstanding contributions in the fields of literature, chemistry, physics, peace and medicine were funded by a legacy and were to be 'annually made to those who, during the preceding year, shall have conferred the greatest benefit on mankind'.

The first recipients in the Science categories were the physicist Wilhelm Conrad Röntgen, for his discovery of X-rays, organic chemist Jacobus H. van't Hoff for his laws of chemical dynamics and, in medicine, German scientist Emil von Behring, who developed a serum against diphtheria and tetanus. The Peace prize went to Red Cross founder, Jean Henri Dunant, and Frederic Passy, founder of the French Society of the Friends of Peace.

BIRTHS

February 28 – Linus Pauling, American chemist and recipient of the 1954 Nobel Prize in Chemistry and Peace.

May 18 – Vincent du Vigneaud, American chemist, 1955 Nobel Prize laureate.

September 29 – Enrico Fermi, Italian physicist, 1938 Nobel Prize laureate.

The Glasgow International Exhibition was visited by 11 million people between May and November, 1901 and celebrated art, machinery and science (Image courtesy of the Estate of Stanley Shoop).

December 5 –Werner Heisenberg, German physicist, 1932 Nobel Prize laureate.

December 16 – Margaret Mead, American cultural anthropologist.

Collectables

Edison Gem Cylinder Phonograph
1901–5 (see Discovering Antiques: Eric Knowles)

Thousands of these machines were made and they are popular with collectors.

First launched in 1878, they work like the gramophone but with the sound cut into grooves on a metal cylinder. Value: £200–£300.

Chapter Three

1902

Politics

NEW PM

ARTHUR JAMES Balfour, First Lord of the Treasury, became Prime Minister, on July 12 following the resignation, due to ill health, of Lord Salisbury. His appointment came just a month before the coronation of the new King.

Lord Salisbury had made Balfour President of the Local Government Board in 1885, and later Secretary for Scotland in 1886, with a seat in the Cabinet. There were those who believed that he owed his success to the fact that he was Lord (Robert) Salisbury's nephew. It has been suggested

Balfour replaced his uncle Lord Salisbury as Prime Minister.

that this gave rise to the popular British expression 'Bob's your uncle' – meaning 'easily fixed'.

Balfour's appointment to Chief Secretary for Ireland in 1897 had raised many eyebrows, but he surprised critics by his steady administration and his uncompromising rejection of Home Rule for Ireland, which earned him the nickname 'Bloody Balfour' amongst Irish nationalists.

EDUCATION ACT

In 1902, the Conservative government introduced a new Education Act that abolished all 2,568 school boards and handed over their duties to Local Education Authorities.

It became a major political issue because the Act integrated denominational schools into the state system, which was supported by taxation. But because the Anglicans had the large majority of denominational schools, nonconformists complained that it was unfair that they should pay for a religious education with which they disagreed.

The nonconformists had a long history of grievances against the British government. Past legislation had excluded them from holding military or civil office, or from being awarded degrees from higher education institutions like Cambridge and Oxford. They had also been forced to pay taxes to contribute to the maintenance of Anglican churches.

Baptist leader John Clifford organised a social movement, the National Passive Resistance Committee, to galvanise opposition. It included Baptists, Methodists, Quakers and Congregationalists. By 1906, over 170 men had gone to prison for refusing to pay their school taxes.

Royalty

CORONATION DRAMA

It was announced on 24 June that the coronation of Edward VII, due to take place in two days' time, had been postponed indefinitely. This was due to him being diagnosed with appendicitis, which required an operation.

The postponement caused a commotion with visiting Royals and dignitaries from abroad. Many had already arrived and were staying at various hotels in London. They suddenly found themselves having to head back home.

On July 6, the King treated the poor of London to dinner and music, to celebrate his accession to the throne. From his sick bed in Buckingham

Land of Hope and Glory - after the initial coronation was cancelled due to ill health, Edward VII returns home from his investiture.

Palace, where he was recovering from his operation, the King sent a message to each local mayor, regretting that he could not be present. The dinners took place at over 700 venues and it is estimated that 456,000 were guests of the monarch.

Thousands volunteered their services for free, over 1,500 entertainers were booked and big breweries were amongst the donators. At the Inns of Court, barristers rolled up their sleeves and washed potatoes and waited on guests.

Edward was eventually crowned at Westminster Abbey on August 9, with the streets lined with well-wishers. Concerns about his health led to a shortened ceremony, and he did not carry the heavy sword of state to the high altar, but remained in his chair.

Two nurses were on standby in the gallery above the Coronation chair but, in the end, it was the Archbishop of Canterbury who was ill. He felt faint and had to retire to a side chapel to rest. The Archbishop later returned to the high altar but was clearly far from well. Having sworn allegiance to his new sovereign on behalf of the clergy of the Church of England, the 80-year-old archbishop had to be helped to his feet. He died four months later.

Kaiser Wilhelm came to Britain to visit his uncle, Edward VII but relations were not good with the German Emperor privately referring to his portly uncle as a 'lying dog'.

THE ORDER OF MERIT

Edward VII established the Order of Merit on June 26, as a reward for distinguished service in the armed forces, science, art, literature, or for the promotion of culture.

Appointments to the Order are in the Sovereign's personal gift and ministerial advice is not required. The Order is limited to the Sovereign and 24 members, but additional foreigners may be added as honorary members.

Historical Events

DEATH OF RHODES

Cecil Rhodes, who gave his name to Rhodesia, died in his cottage near Cape Town on March 26, aged 48.

Cecil Rhodes died on 26th March, he was only 48 but he left an impressive legacy. Rhodesia, now Zimbabwe, was named after him. Recipients of the Rhodes Scholarship which the Rhodes Trust established in 1904 for international students to study at Oxford include President Bill Clinton and Australian Prime Minister Bob Hawke.

The British-born businessman, imperialist and politician amassed a fortune in South Africa by consolidating diamond mining. He was the founder of the diamond company De Beers.

A fervent believer of colonialism, he used his wealth and power to advance the interests of the British Empire, and he became Prime Minister of the Cape in 1890.

The end of the Second Boer War (1899-1902) was a time of celebration and mourning as 20,000 British troops never returned home.

VOLCANIC ERUPTION KILLS THOUSANDS

There was huge loss of life in one of the worst volcano eruptions of the century. On May 8, Mount Pelée, on the island of Martinique erupted, destroying the main town of St Pierre and killing over 30,000 people.

The eruptions began on April 25, when rocks and ashes were emitted. Further eruptions occurred in the following days, sending a film of ash below, but no one was unduly worried.

As the activity intensified, some people decided to evacuate. Panic spread when part of the crater collapsed, sending mud below, which buried around 150 people. But while many people were intent on leaving St Pierre, many more from the countryside were attempting to find refuge in the city, increasing its population by several thousand.

The main eruption devastated about eight square miles, with St Pierre taking the brunt. There were pitifully few survivors.

BOERS SURRENDER

Boer leaders arrived in Pretoria to meet Lord Milner, the High Commissioner, and Lord Kitchener, the Commander-in-Chief, to sign terms of surrender on May 31. After two years and seven months of fighting, the Boer War was finally over.

The treaty ended the existence of Transvaal and the Orange Free State as independent Boer republics and placed them within the British Empire. But the Boers were promised eventual limited self-government.

DISCOVERY EXPEDITION

On December 31, explorer Robert Falcon Scott and Dr Edward Wilson arrived at the furthest southern point that had been reached by man at 82° 17'S.

They were part of the National Antarctic Expedition, which was organised by the Royal Geographical Society. The team had left Dundee, aboard the ship D*iscovery*, on July 31 1901, bound for Antarctica. Because of this, it became commonly known as the Discovery Expedition.

The centrepiece of the expedition was an attempt to reach the South Pole, or at least to explore further south than anyone had managed to do previously. The core party was Scott, Wilson and third lieutenant Ernest Shackleton, who did not reach as far south as the other two because he was ordered to stay and look after the dogs.

Scott and Shackleton were to become keen rivals in following years.

Dr Edward Wilson was part of Robert Scott's Discovery Expedition and would be part of Captain Scott's ill-fated South Pole Expedition a decade later.

Social Change

THE PEOPLE OF THE ABYSS

In 1902, American Jack London arrived in London's East End to research a book on living conditions in the slums. He swapped his clothes for threadbare second-hand ones, adopted the identity of a stranded sailor and began to gather a huge amount of information and material.

The People of the Abyss, which also included pictures taken by London, was to become a hugely important social document. He discovered that the residents of the slum areas were not there through choice, or idleness, but through disease, disability or old age, resulting in an inability to work for decent wages.

In the following passage, London described the living conditions for the families condemned to live in the area:

'Not only was one room deemed sufficient for a poor man and his family, but I learned that many families, occupying single rooms, had so much space to spare as to be able to take in a lodger or two.

'When such rooms can be rented for from three to six shillings per week, it is a fair conclusion that a lodger with references should obtain floor space for, say, from eightpence to a shilling.'

On childhood in the area, the author commented:

'There is one beautiful sight in the East End, and only one, and it is the children dancing in the street when the organ-grinder goes his round.'

Although he found the children were as bright and imaginative as any others, he concluded that their lives were destined to be blighted by degradation, disease and even death.

'The outlook for children is hopeless. They die like flies, and those that survive, survive because they possess excessive vitality and a capacity of adaptation to the degradation with which they are surrounded.

'They have no home life. In the dens and lairs in which they live they are exposed to all that is obscene and indecent. And as their minds are made rotten, so are their bodies made rotten by bad sanitation, overcrowding, and underfeeding.

'When a father and mother live with three or four children in a room where the children take turn about in sitting up to drive the rats away from the sleepers, when those children never have enough to eat and are preyed upon and made miserable and weak by swarming vermin, the sort of men and women the survivors will make can readily be imagined.'

LICENSING ACT 1902

In an attempt to tackle drunkenness in the working classes, Parliament passed a new licensing law which gave police the power to arrest anyone who was drunk and incapable, and outlawed the sale of alcohol to 'habitual drunkards'. Crucially, it also made it a criminal offence to be drunk in charge of a child, which was not uncommon in the poorer districts.

BIRTH OF A SOCIAL WORKER

Dame Eileen Younghusband, an early pioneer of social work in the UK, was born in January. Her early life in Westerham, Kent, and in India was a privileged one but at 22, at the suggestion of a friend, she decided to help the less fortunate by becoming a social worker. Through her work she got to know the women and children of Bermondsey and Stepney, and felt that more should be done to help them.

She went on to become a lecturer at the London School of Economics, while devoting her spare time to the Citizens' Advice Bureau, the Bermondsey Settlement and women refugees.

In 1955, she chaired a working party about the role of social workers and was instrumental in the regulation of training. Six years later, she helped set up the National Institute for Social Work Training. Dame Eileen died in a car accident, during a US lecture tour, shortly before her eighttieth birthday.

Fashion

FIT FOR A KING

Just as his wife, Queen Alexandra, led the way in ladies' dress, King Edward VII was a huge influence on men's fashion. His dapper style made the wearing of Homburg hats fashionable, and his hunting attire led to a boom in tweed and single-breasted Norfolk jackets.

For formal meals, Edward VII introduced the custom of black tie and dinner jacket, rather than white tie and tails, and he was also the first to wear trousers pressed from seam to seam, rather than creased down the middle.

By the time of his coronation, Edward VII had become quite a portly figure, with a waist measurement of 48 inches (122cm). As a result, he would leave the bottom button of his suit jacket unbuttoned and this sparked a tradition which is still visible today.

His career as a trendsetter began in 1846 when, at the age of four, he was given a miniature version of the uniform worn by sailors on the Royal Yacht. The fame of the sailor suit spread and, by 1870, had become one of the most popular outfits for little boys.

PARIS COMES TO LONDON

In 1902, Madame Paquin, the first successful woman designer in haute couture, brought her wares to London.

She opened her salon in 39 Dover Street with the advertising slogan, 'Each creation original and produced in Paris and London simultaneous'. Her stunning designs were an instant hit with fashionable London ladies and she counted the Queen among her customers.

Her expansion continued in latter years, when she opened stores in Buenos Aires and Madrid.

Entertainment

FILM

The first special effects were used by former stage magician Georges Melies. Since the inception of cinema five years earlier, the novelty of watching everyday events, such as workers leaving a factory, on the big screen was wearing off. The Melies film *A Trip to the Moon* depicted a rocket travelling through space, strange aliens and the spectacle of the moon's animated face being struck in the eye with the rocket.

Huge crowds gathered to watch the film, which marked a new progression in the art of cinema.

On April 2, the first US cinema opened in Los Angeles. *Electric Theater* was the brainchild of Thomas L. Tally, who had previously been showing short films in the back of his amusement parlour. Sadly, as audiences became indifferent to the magic of moving films, their numbers declined.

The same was happening everywhere. One projectionist from New York reported that film had, at first, attracted 'crowded houses on account of its novelty. Now everybody has seen it, and, to use the vernacular of the "foyer," it does not "draw flies"'. The Electric Theatre converted to a Vaudeville venue six months after opening.

In Britain, film-maker Will Barker created the first UK studio when he bought four acres of land containing a large house and a lodge in North London, and began to use it as a setting for his movies. Five years later, he was to move the whole operation to West London – and name it Ealing Studios.

THEATRE

In April, the Irish National Theatre was formed by poet W.B. Yeats, Lady Gregory, J.M. Synge and George Russell.

In October, the society produced Yeats' openly nationalistic play *Cathleen ni Houlihan*, which portrayed Ireland as an old lady asking for her four fields to be returned to her. When Irish men agree to fight on her behalf, she is transformed into a young beauty.

The lead was taken by Yeats' muse, Maud Gonne, a militant Irish nationalist, with whom he was in unrequited love and who is the subject of many of his poems. A year later, on marrying John McBride in Paris, Maud plotted to assassinate Edward VII using their honeymoon in Spain as a cover. King Edward VII visited Gibraltar at the time but, in the end, the assassination attempt was aborted.

On the London stage, Elleline Terriss and Seymour Hicks were starring in Hicks' plays *The Cherry Girl* and *Quality Street*. The golden couple, who had married in 1893, moved to a new home in Surrey in 1902 and the success of their play was such that the cul-de-sac that they moved to was renamed *Quality Street*.

Gordon Craig's costume design for the Purcell Society's revivals of Handel's *Acis and Galatea* and Purcell's *Masque of Love* gained world-wide notoriety. *The New York Times* reported that the outfits 'cause much pleasantry, all dresses being made of loose strips of tape and ribbon, and

Sarah Bernhardt was one of the greatest actresses of the century but her row with playwright Catulle Mendes showed a fiery side to her nature.

bearing as little likeness to any clothes ever worn on the face of this planet as the most advanced artist could desire'.

J.M Barrie wrote *The Admirable Chrichton* and, in Paris, beautiful actress Sarah Bernhardt had a furious row with playwright Catulle Mendes over his withdrawal from the play *Saint Therese*, which she had been producing. The row played out in an increasingly bitter volley of letters which M. Mendes then published.

In response, Miss Bernhardt published a letter which stated 'I came out of this crisis a physical wreck with my brain a whirl, but my will safe and sound. As long as I live, I will never see Catulle Mendes again.'

MUSIC

Italian operatic tenor Enrico Caruso made his first gramophone recording and became one of the pioneers of recorded music.

His popular recordings and his extraordinary voice, known for its range and power, made him one of the best-known stars of his time.

Caruso was one of the first star vocalists to make numerous recordings. He and the disc phonograph did much to promote each other in the first two decades of the Twentieth Century.

His first recordings, made in 1902, were for the Gramophone and Typewriter Company. They went on to sell millions worldwide.

BIRTHS

January 31 – Tallulah Bankhead, actress.
March   28 – Flora Robson, actress.
March   10 – David O. Selznick, producer.
May 2 – Brian Aherne, stage and screen actor.
August   10 – Norma Shearer, actress.
September 5 – Darryl F. Zanuck, producer, screenwriter, director.
October 5 – Larry Fine, actor, comedian, member of The Three Stooges
December 9 – Margaret Hamilton, actress (Wicked Witch of the West in *The Wizard of Oz*).
December 19 – Ralph Richardson, stage and screen actor.

Literature

ZOLA DIES

In September, French writer Emile Zola was killed by fumes from a blocked chimney at his Paris home. The author, whose works included *Germinal* and *Nana,* had gained many political enemies when he defended a Jewish army captain who was jailed on trumped up charges. Zola published an open letter entitled *J'accuse,* which blamed the French president for the miscarriage of justice, and was later convicted of criminal libel. He fled to England to avoid jail but returned to France when the government fell.

At 9 am on September 29, a servant found the writer and his wife overcome by fumes in their home. Mme Zola survived but it was too late for her 62-year-old husband. Decades later, a Parisian roofer claimed, on his deathbed, to have blocked the chimney for political reasons.

Beatrix Potter's Peter Rabbit has delighted children for generations and sparked a wealth of collectables, including this Wedgwood porringer.

PETER RABBIT IS BORN

Beatrix Potter's *The Tale of Peter Rabbit* was published. The author illustrated the story of a mischievous bunny with her own watercolours. Potter had begun drawing wildlife pictures on family holidays in the Lake District as a child, and was encouraged to put them in book form by publisher and friend Frederick Warne. *The Tale of Peter Rabbit* has sold over 40 million copies worldwide and was the first of 24 stories by the talented author.

SHERLOCK AND FRIENDS

Arthur Conan Doyle published the Sherlock Holmes mystery *The Hounds of the Baskervilles* in book form, having already serialised it in *The Strand* magazine. While writing the novel, Doyle was working as a doctor in Plymouth and set the story on nearby Dartmoor, where he often walked.

Other literary works published this year included Joseph Conrad's disturbing *Heart of Darkness*, Rudyard Kipling's *Just So Stories* and Henry James' *The Wings of a Dove*.

Rudyard Kipling's classic *Just So Stories* have thrilled generations of children.

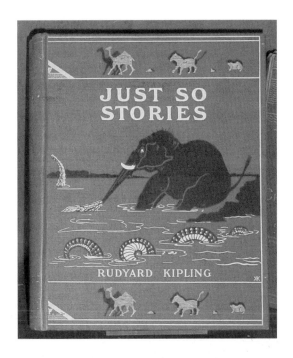

BIRTHS

Jan 5 – Stella Gibbons, novelist.
Feb 27 – John Steinbeck, writer, Nobel Prize laureate.
August 16 – Georgette Heyer, novelist.
August 19 – Ogden Nash, poet.

DEATHS

September 29 – Emile Zola, French author.

Architecture

TURIN EXHIBITION

Following the success of the 1900 Exposition Universelle in Paris, the Italian city of Turin played host to a similar event, which opened in May. The 'First International Exhibition of Modern Decorative Art' was restricted to innovative art and architecture which was not influenced by past works.

It also followed the Art Nouveau concept of complete design, as this extract from the ruling shows:

'The Exhibition will include artistic manifestations and products concerning the aesthetic of the 'street' as well as those of the house and of the room.

'The only products that will be allowed will be original ones that show a true intent of aesthetic renewal of the shape. We will not accept simple imitations of styles of the past, nor industrial production not inspired by an artistic ideal.'

Scottish architect Charles Rennie Mackintosh rose to the challenge by designing the Scottish Pavilion and filling it with his creations. The critical acclaim he received led to exhibitions in Venice, Munich, Dresden and Moscow.

Carlo Bugatti was another successful exhibitor in Turin. The Italian architect created three rooms of furniture, including the Cobra Chair, which boasted a seat and back formed in one continuous curve and pre-empted the Art Deco style of the 1920s. The Turin jury awarded him a 'diploma of honour' for his radical designs.

COLLAPSE OF ST MARK'S CAMPANILE

St Mark's Campanile, the imposing bell tower of St Mark's Basilica in Venice, collapsed on July 14.

The north wall of the tower had begun to show signs of a dangerous crack days earlier which continued to grow. Finally, the campanile collapsed completely. Remarkably, no one was killed. That same evening, the communal council approved 500,000 Lire for the reconstruction of the campanile. It was to be rebuilt as it had been, but with some internal reinforcement to prevent future collapse.

ASWAN DAM

In Egypt, the Nile dame Aswan was completed in December, after four years of construction work by 11,000 builders. Built to reserve some of the annual flood waters for the dry summer spells, for use in agricultural irrigation, it was a massive one and a quarter miles long and 130 feet high.

NANCY

A group of artists and architects known as L'ecole de Nancy, formed by Emile Galle, had turned the French town of Nancy into a cultural centre to rival Paris.

Working in the Art Nouveau style, they designed many public buildings which earned Nancy the name of 'Capitale de l'Est'.

In 1902, the buildings designed in the city included Villa Lejeune, France-Lanord and the Lombard Apartment Buildings, all by Émile André. Also the Biet Apartment Buildings, designed by George Biet and Eugène Vallin.

Art

WORLD'S LARGEST MODERN ART EXHIBITION

Turin was selected as the site of the largest exhibition of modern decorative arts ever staged.

Amongst the eye-catching displays at the Turin Exhibition were four rooms decorated by Carlo Bugatti from Milan, an artist who worked in an eccentric style influenced by Asian and North African designs.

The main idea of the Exhibition was that decorative arts embraced many aspects, from the everyday tool to urban 'furniture', from the gate of a villa to the most luxurious hotel. Design was a complete activity which spanned every aspect of production from doorknobs to coffee cups.

CUBIST ARTIST BEGIN STUDIES

French painter and sculptor Georges Braque began his studies at the Academie Humbert in Paris, where he was to meet Marie Laurencin and Francis Picabia.

Braque, along with Pablo Picasso, later developed the art movement known as Cubism.

MODERN ART GALLERY IN VENICE

The Galleria Internazionale d'Arte Moderna opened in Venice, in the Ca' Pesaro, a sixteenth-century palace on the Grand Canal.

The gallery was founded in 1897 by Prince Alberto Giovannelli, at which time the art was displayed at Ca' Foscari. The collection was moved to Ca' Pesaro on May 18 1902.

Travel and Transport

ANTARCTIC BALLOON

British explorers, Robert Falcon Scott and Ernest Shackleton, made the first balloon flight in Antarctica, on February 4. They ascended to 244 metres in a tethered hydrogen balloon to take the first Antarctic aerial photographs.

DID IT FLY?

American aviation pioneer Lyman Gilmore claimed that he had flown his steam-powered airplane over a field in Grass Valley, California, on May 15. This would make him the first person to fly a powered airplane.

However, the incident cannot be verified. Although there are photographs from 1898 showing Gilmore's machine, there are none showing the plane in the air.

HITTING THE BUFFERS

A serious buffer stop collision at Frankfurt am Main, Germany, led to the invention of a new energy-absorbing type.

The large mass of a train, even at low speed, transfers a sizeable amount of energy when it collides with a buffer stop as it arrives at the railway station. But by using hydraulics, the energy was dissipated and so the train came to a more gradual and safer halt.

US CAR GIANTS GET INTO GEAR

In the US, the stirrings began of what were to become famous worldwide vehicle manufacturers.

In 1901, John Francis Dodge and Horace Elgin Dodge moved their Dodge Brothers Bicycle & Machine Factory from Windsor, Ontario to Detroit, Michigan. It was there that their auto parts were most in demand with the early automobile industry, including the Olds Motor Vehicle Company, which was mass marketing the popular Oldsmobiles.

In 1902, the Dodge brothers were approached by Henry Ford, who was looking for help in financing his own company.

CAR USERS RALLY

The American Automobile Association was founded on March 4, in response to a lack of highways suitable for autos. It also united drivers against widespread public disapproval of the automobile and its noise.

GETTING IT WRIGHT

Wilbur and Orville Wright developed their third and most successful glider to date. It had a 32-foot wing-span and they began testing it at Kitty Hawk, North Carolina, on September 19.
Over the next five weeks, they made between 700 and 1000 glide flights. The longest of these was 622.5 ft in 26 seconds.

BIRTHS

February 4 – US aviator Charles Lindbergh, who made the first solo, non-stop flight across the Atlantic.

Toys

THE BIRTH OF THE TEDDY BEAR

In November, President Theodore 'Teddy' Roosevelt was on a hunting expedition when he failed to kill a bear. His companions, wishing to please him, caught and tethered a bear cub but the President refused to kill it. 'Spare the Bear,' he is said to have ordered. 'I will not shoot a tethered animal.'

A cartoon depicting the incident was published in the *Washington Post* and the *Washington Evening Star*, and became the unlikely inspiration for one of the most enduring toys in the world.

Brooklyn shopkeepers Morris and Rose Michtom made a toy bear which they named 'Teddy's bear' and displayed in their window, along with the cartoon. They went on to make a fortune manufacturing bears with the Ideal Novelty and Toy Company.

At the same time, the first jointed bear was being designed by Richard Steiff, in Germany. The nephew of Steiff founder Margarete, he displayed his creation at the Leipzig toy fair in 1903 and the popularity of teddy bears quickly spread through Europe as well as the US.

On hearing of the new craze, in 1903, the US President commented 'I don't think my name is likely to be worth much in the toy bear business, but you are welcome to use it.'

Sport

IBROX DISASTER

Twenty six people died and 500 were injured when a stand collapsed at the Ibrox Park stadium in Glasgow during an England-Scotland football match on April 5.

Around 80,000 supporters were packed into the overcrowded stadium and disaster struck soon after kick-off. A section of terracing at the top of one end of the grandstand collapsed, leaving a great hole 20 yards square. Hundreds of spectators fell 40 feet to the ground below. Others were crushed underfoot as panicking fans fled onto the pitch.

Mounted police, thinking there was a pitch invasion, rode into the fleeing crowd to stop them. Incredibly, most of the crowd was unaware of the seriousness of the accident, and the match continued even as the dead and injured were being carried from the stadium.

The disaster discredited the practice of supporting terracing on steel frames. Subsequently, British sports grounds were built with terracing formed on earth embankments or reinforced concrete.

FIRST MOTOR RACE IN THE UK

The first motor race in the UK was held in Bexhill-on-Sea on 19 May, organised by the Automobile Club of Great Britain and Ireland. It attracted international attention.

Automobiles were gaining in popularity but the first car race did not prove popular with all and a property owner effectively banned future car races in Bexhill.

Hosted by the eighth Earl De La Warr, it was part of a campaign to promote Bexhill-on-Sea as a fashionable new resort. The Earl's interest in motorcars was also linked to his association with the firm Dunlop, of which he was chairman.

The event was run along a one-kilometre track, with a flying start from the top of Galley Hill.

The races were deemed to have been a great success, and more events were planned for later in 1902 and in 1903. However, the excitement was cut short when Mr Mayner, a property owner on De La Warr Parade, took out an injunction against the Earl. This banned all future motor racing.

BIRTHS

January 16 – Eric Liddell, Scottish runner, Olympic champion, immortalised in the film *Chariots of Fire*.
March 17 – Bobby Jones of the US, acclaimed as the greatest ever amateur golfer.

The Home

TELEPHONES

A quarter of a century after Alexander Graham Bell invented the telephone, more and more people had one in their homes. But progress had been slow in the UK, compared to the faster advancements in the US and, until the turn of the century, it was mainly rich businesses who had possessed the new gadget.

However, newer, less cumbersome handsets, which no longer required a large battery in the cellar, led to many upper and middle class homes joining the trend. By 1902, there were seven telephone exchanges in London.

In some provinces, local councils were granted the right to run their own telephone exchanges, in competition with those of the National Telephone Company. Glasgow and Tunbridge Wells did so in 1901 and Swansea and Portsmouth followed suit in 1902, but were quick to find that profits were hard to come by, reverting back to the national scheme in years to come.

The Hull Corporation also gained its licence in 1902 and remains the only telephone exchange in the control of a local authority.

The Changing Role of Women

ROSA LEWIS

At a time when class division and suppression of women defined society, the story of Rosa Lewis is an inspiration. She was born in Essex, the daughter of a working class tradesman, and went into domestic service as a young girl. She worked her way up the servants' ranks and became the head of the kitchen for the wealthy Duke of Orleans.

Having learned French cuisine, she began a cooking service for rich households which was soon to become so popular that she had to employ teams of cooks to help her. Her fame spread, and she even cooked for King Edward VII, who was said to be impressed.

By 1902, she had made enough money to buy her own hotel – 'the Cavendish' in Jermyn Street. It soon became one of the most exclusive hotels in London and earned her the nickname, The Duchess of Jermyn Street.

BARMAIDS' VICTORY

In April, magistrates in Glasgow banned barmaids from licensed premises in an attempt to preserve morality and good order. They argued that women should not be subjected to the sort of language and suggestive treatment that was common in pubs, and refused to renew licences for employers who flouted the ban.

Restaurateur Daniel Brown was the only employer to appeal. On May 12, the Appeal Court decision overturned the decision and granted him a licence.

THE FIGHT FOR RIGHTS

On February 18, a delegation of female textile workers from the North of England travelled to London with a petition which demanded votes for women. The document, signed by 37,000, was presented to Parliament.

In Australia, women were granted the right to vote for the first time.

MIDWIVES

After 20 years of successful campaigning by the 'Midwives' Institute', parliament passed the Midwives' Act for England and Wales. The act regulated the training and practice of midwives and made it illegal for anyone who was unqualified to act as a midwife.

Science

CARNEGIE INSTITUTION

Millionaire businessman and philanthropist Andrew Carnegie founded the Carnegie Institution of Washington as an organisation for scientific discovery, with a $10 million donation. His intention was for the institution to be home to exceptional individuals – men and women with imagination and extraordinary dedication capable of working at the cutting edge of their fields.

EDISON'S BATTERY

Thomas Edison invented a new and more efficient battery on May 28. The electrical storage battery, consisting of nickel and iron in an alkaline solution, was lighter than the lead-acid type and lasted longer.

NEON LAMP INVENTED

French engineer, chemist, and inventor Georges Claude became the first to apply an electrical discharge to a sealed tube of neon gas to create a

Neon lamps were a sign of the future, as announced in *The Strand Magazine* which created a neon-like Happy Christmas sign.

lamp. The word neon comes from the Greek 'neos,' meaning 'the new gas'. Georges Claude displayed the first neon lamp to the public on December 11, 1910, in Paris.

MALARIA BREAKTHROUGH

Major Ronald Ross was awarded the Nobel Prize for medicine for his work on the causes of malaria.

His discovery, that the deadly disease is transmitted by the bite of a female mosquito, was a major advance in the search for a cure.

Born in Almora, India, the son of General Sir C.C.G. Ross of the British Army, Ross studied medicine at St Bartholomew's Hospital in London. He joined the Indian Medical Service in 1881, where he studied malaria and discovered the presence of the malarial parasite within a specific species of mosquito, the Anopheles.

Later, he demonstrated that malaria is transmitted from infected birds to healthy ones by the bite of a mosquito, a finding that suggested the disease's mode of transmission to humans.

In 1902, he was awarded the Nobel Prize for his work and was appointed a Companion of the Most Honourable Order of Bath by King Edward VII.

FIRST TEA-MAKING MACHINE

Probably the first commercially produced. automatic tea-making machine was built by Albert E. Richardson, a clockmaker from Ashton-under-Lyne, Lancashire.

This remarkable device comprised a wooden base which held an alarm clock, kettle tilter and methylated spirit stove, with a flat oval-shaped copper kettle.

Once the clock had reached a pre-set time, the winder released a catch allowing an arm to spring back and strike a match which was held against some abrasive paper by spring pressure. The match then lit a spirit lamp positioned under the kettle.

Steam from boiling water would lift a plate, tipping the kettle forward, pouring the water into a cup.

Once the kettle had tipped up sufficiently it, released another catch which allowed a shutter to slide over the spirit lamp to extinguish it. As the shutter slid across, it moved an arm, which struck the bell on top of the clock, to wake the lucky person with a hot cup of tea or coffee.

The original machine, and all rights to it, were purchased from

Richardson by the Birmingham gunsmith Frank Clarke, who patented it on April 7 1902 calling it 'An Apparatus Whereby a Cup of Tea or Coffee is Automatically Made'.

He marketed the tea-maker to his rich clients.

THE FIRST AIR-CONDITIONING

New Yorker Willis Haviland Carrier invented the first air conditioning, although it was then known as an 'Apparatus for Treating Air'.

Carrier worked as an engineer at the Buffalo Forge Company, designing heating systems to dry lumber and coffee. In 1902, he devised a system to control heat and humidity for the Sackett-Wilhelms Lithographing and Publishing Company in Brooklyn. The firm had been unable to print reliable colours because of the effects of heat and humidity on paper and ink. The new air-conditioning machine created a stable environment. Carrier later set up his own company and amassed a fortune from his invention.

BIRTHS

July 28 – Karl Popper, generally regarded as one of the greatest philosophers of science of the Twentieth Century.

Chapter Four

1903

Politics

POMP AND CEREMONY IN DELHI

LORD CURZON, the Viceroy of India, instigated two weeks of festivities full of pomp and finery at the end of the previous year to commemorate Edward VII as the new Emperor of India.

The events culminated in the official ceremony on January 1, when Lord Curzon, sitting on a regal gold and white dais, signalled the trumpets to sound whilst a lone horseman rode up and read a proclamation. Lord Curzon then read a message from the new Emperor and announced that there would be a remission of interest on British loans for those states suffering from famine.

PANAMA CANAL

The US and the Republic of Colombia signed a treaty on January 22, allowing for the construction of a Panama Canal.

The Colombian government credited the US the right to build a canal and a strip of land six miles wide, in exchange for an annual rental and a sum in gold. The project had keen support from President Roosevelt who believed that a U.S-controlled canal across Central America was of vital strategic interest to his country.

Indeed, the potential of a water passage between North and South America was recognised by the earliest colonists of Central America, and schemes for such a canal were floated several times in the subsequent years.

An initial attempt by France to build a sea-level canal failed, but only after a great amount of excavation was carried out. This was to prove beneficial to the US engineers when they began work.

DEATH OF LORD SALISBURY

Lord Salisbury, four times Tory Prime Minister, died on August 22 at the age of 73. He had suffered from a weak heart and had retired as PM the previous year. His nephew and successor Arthur Balfour was by his bedside when he passed away.

Telegrams of tribute arrived in London from all over Europe. The funeral, on August 31, was a private affair at the Cecil family home of Hatfield, in Hertfordshire, with just family, a few intimate neighbours and tenants and staff present. The coffin was carried to and from the parish church by family retainers.

The Archbishop of Canterbury officiated at the funeral service, and Lord Salisbury was buried beside his wife in the burial ground on his estate. The King and Queen sent wreaths, as did other European Royalty.

Simultaneously, a memorial service was held in Westminster Abbey, attended by dignitaries and politicians.

SPLIT IN RUSSIAN POLITICAL PARTY

At a stormy congress in London on November 17, the Russian Social Democratic Labour Party split into two distinct groups – the Bolsheviks ('majority') and Mensheviks ('minority').

The Bolsheviks, under Vladimir Lenin, believed that a revolution must be led by a single centralised party of professional revolutionaries. The opposing Mensheviks, led by Yuly Martov, advocated a broad proletarian party.

CHAMBERLAIN RESIGNS

Joseph Chamberlain, the Colonial Secretary, resigned from the Cabinet on September 17 after eight years. He quit office in order to have greater freedom in advocating preferential tariff treatment for Empire countries.

Joseph Chamberlain resigned as the Colonial Secretary. Whilst never elected as Prime Minister, his political influence and reputation cannot be underestimated. His son, Neville, became Prime Minister and is most famous for his naïve 'Peace for our time' speech.

Royalty

KING ASSASSINATED

King Alexander of Serbia and his wife Queen Draga were brutally murdered in their palace.

The monarch had aroused anger in 1900 when he suddenly announced his engagement to the widow Madame Draga Mašin, formerly a lady-in-waiting to his mother Queen Natalie.

His father, Milan, who had unexpectedly abdicated in 1809 in favour of his son, was furious, and his mother's strong opposition prompted Alexander to ban her from the palace.

They married in 1900, but the King was to anger politicians and the military again when it was rumoured that he was about to proclaim one of the two unpopular brothers of Queen Draga, Lieutenant Nikodije, as heir-apparent to the throne. The choice of the government, in the advent of a childless marriage, was Prince Mirko of Montenegro who was married to Natalija Konstantinovic, the granddaughter of Princess Anka Obrenovi, the aunt of King Milan.

Conspirators plotted to kill the King and a group of disaffected army officers stormed the palace on the morning of June 11, 1903. They found the royal couple hiding in a cupboard in their bedroom and shot them both. Prince Mirko was subsequently crowned King Peter I.

Historical Events

PLAGUE IN INDIA

The Bubonic Plague which had ravaged India since the outbreak in Bombay in 1896, claimed a staggering 850,000 lives in 1903 alone.

The climate and the unsanitary conditions of the outlying districts and native sections of the towns, made it difficult to control the epidemic, which broke out continually at fresh points throughout the country.

TIDAL WAVE STRIKES POLYNESIA

Thousands died after a huge tidal wave swept through the Polynesian islands of Society and Tuamoto on January 13.

ARCHBISHOP APPOINTED

Dr Randall Davidson became Archbishop of Canterbury on February 12. Born in Edinburgh in 1848, he was educated at Harrow and Trinity College, Oxford. He became chaplain to Queen Victoria and served as Dean of Windsor, the Bishop of Rochester and Bishop of Winchester.

'MAD MULLAH' TAKEN SERIOUSLY

Following fresh outbreaks of fighting in Somaliland, the British sent extra troops to deal with the man they had once dismissed as the 'Mad Mullah'.

The Mullah, Mohammed Abdullah Hasan, claimed to possess super-natural powers. He certainly was a skilful orator and poet who gained many followers with stirring words, claiming that the British infidels 'have destroyed our religion and made our children their children'. Christian Ethiopians also came under attack for 'plundering the political and religious freedom of the Somali nation'.

The Mullah and his followers attacked and ransacked many tribes who refused to accept the idea of Somali unity and independence.

Heavy fighting between the 'dervishes' and the British was to continue throughout the year.

DEATH OF POPE

Pope Leo XIII died at the age of 93 on July 20, after a 25-year period in office. Known as the 'Pope of the Working Man', he worked to unite Christendom and to reduce class warfare. He was succeeded by Pope Pius X on August 4.

THOUSANDS MASSACRED

Turkish troops massacred thousands of Bulgarian men, women and children in the village of Monastir on September 8, in retaliation for a decision by the Macedonian Central Revolutionary Committee to mount a revolt against Turkish rule.

Social Change

COTTON SHORTAGE

A worldwide cotton shortage led to closures of cotton mills throughout Britain. A report, published on August 22, stated that Manchester had been particularly badly hit, while a local newspaper in Macclesfield reported that job losses there had reached crisis point.

'Owing to the shortage of cotton, 1,000 operatives at Macclesfield have been thrown out of work for the past three months. Arrangements for the relief of the distressed work people has been started and we may expect, with the characteristic generosity of the British public, the pressing of this untoward state of things will be relieved.'

CHILD TRADERS

The Employment of Children Act gave local authorities the power to make bye-laws governing the minimum age of street traders. There was an absolute ban on children under 11 selling wares on the street and it became illegal for those between 11 and 16 to work at night.

The Act defined street trading as 'the hawking of newspapers, matches, flowers, and other articles, playing, singing, or performing for profit, shoe-blacking, or any other like occupation carried on in streets or public places'.

Selling of newspapers before 7 am was outlawed, but the delivery by paper boys and girls was allowed.

HEALTH AND HOUSING

With many social reformers concentrating their efforts on the appalling housing conditions of the poor, slum housing was steadily being cleared for new houses to be built, but progress was slow.

In his report, *Survey of Life and Labour in London*, Charles Booth described the squalor of London's houses, saying, 'Those who can afford it move out; those who cannot crowd in.'

The Conservatives set up a Royal Commission to enquire into the work-ings of the Poor Law and an inter-departmental Committee on Physical Deterioration. Their remit was to investigate whether the health of the British people was declining, and to examine poor housing and living conditions.

On October 26, the foundation stone was laid for the new Royal Waterloo Hospital for Women and Children. The original hospital had been built in 1823, but had initially been used by those who could pay for their medical services. In 1851, a trust was set up to allow a small number of poor women to receive treatment. Between 1903 and 1905, the five-storey, red-brick hospital, which still stands on the site next to Waterloo Bridge, was built.

PESPI-COLA

On June 16, the year-old Pepsi-Cola company registered its trade name Pepsi-Cola. The drink had been sold as 'Brad's drink' by Caleb Bradham in his North Carolina drug store for ten years, and had been renamed after the pepsin and cola nuts used to make it. When it was registered in 1903, it was advertised as 'Exhilarating, Invigorating, Aids Digestion'. A mighty 7,968 gallons of the syrup was sold to pharmacies that year.

Fashion

POIRET THE LIBERATOR

Although his most revolutionary design was not to emerge until five years later, French couturier Paul Poiret opened his first fashion house in 1903, on Rue Auber.

Born in Paris in 1879, his first job was with the house of Doucet as an assistant draughtsman to Jacques Doucet, and he went on to work with the world famous House of Worth, founded by Englishman Charles Worth.

Branching out by himself, Poiret brought an exotic influence to his outfits, which were inspired by his love of the India and the East.

His designs were sumptuous and colourful, worked in silk and brocade with gold embroidery. In 1908, he would change the face of fashion with his 'hobble skirt', liberating the previously constricted female waist with a new style of corset. In 1910, he caused more controversy with his daring Harem trousers.

The first designer to launch a signature scent, which he named after his daughter Rosine, Poiret is now considered one of the most influential designers of the Twentieth Century.

Christian Dior, writing in 1955, said 'this great artist excelled at creation and decoration. His models were vigorous sketches, whereas the fussy toilettes of his predecessors had been carefully painted miniatures.'

Entertainment

MUSIC AND DANCE

By 1903, the advent of recorded sound had moved on from the paper cylinders pioneered by Edison and was now being manufactured on flat discs. In 1903, Thomas Edison's own company and arch rivals the Columbia Company began to manufacture regular recordings of new music. Popular discs included *Any Rags*, by Arthur Collins, and *Haiwatha*, by Edison Grand Concert Band.

Also in this year, the first 12' (30 cm) discs were produced and edible records, made from chocolate, became a culinary treat.

THEATRE

January 20 saw the Broadway opening of *The Wizard of Oz*, after a successful run at the Grand Opera House in Chicago. Adapted by L. Frank Baum from his classic novel, it was produced by Fred Hamlin with music by Paul Tietjens.

Unlike the book, the play focused on the Tin Man and Scarecrow, played by Vaudeville team David Montgomery and Fred Stone, rather than Dorothy. It was a huge hit, becoming the longest-running show of the decade, with 290 performances. As a response to the play's popularity, subsequent editions of the book, *The Wonderful Wizard of Oz*, were renamed with the shorter title.

In Chicago, tragedy struck at a packed pantomime at the Iroquois Theatre. On December 30, during a Saturday Matinee of *Mr Bluebeard*, starring Eddie Foy, a piece of scenery caught fire and within minutes the blaze was out of control. The exits were blocked and the audience panicked, resulting in over 600 deaths.

FILM

The flagging interest in the cinematic experience was somewhat revived by the arrival of *The Great Train Robbery*, the first narrative action film, which opened on June 15. Directed and photographed by Edwin S. Porter, it was based on a real hold-up in Wyoming in August 1900, when George Leroy Parker (better known as Butch Cassidy) and his 'Hole in the Wall Gang' held up the Number Three train on the Union Pacific Railroad .

The infamous outlaws forced the conductor to separate the passenger

The Great Train Robbery lasted for an action-packed but silent eight minutes.

cars from the rest of the train, and then blew up a safe in the mail car, escaping with $5,000 cash.

Although set in Wyoming, the film was shot at Thomas Edison's New York studio and along the Lackawanna railroad in New Jersey.

After an action-packed eight minutes, the film climaxed with a bandit firing a pistol out at the audience. The scene caused a sensation, with audiences flocking back again and again to repeat the experience; the film was a huge commercial success. Once again, film-makers began to see movies as a viable enterprise.

In September, the first cowboy film, *Kit Carson*, was screened. Based on the life of the legendary frontiersman, it showed Kit and his colleagues battling with savage American Indians before he is captured and taken to their settlement. Taunted and beaten, Kit's salvation comes in the form of an Indian squaw who takes pity on him and releases him. The film ends with a touching reunion between Kit his wife and child.

BIRTHS

February 26 – Vincente Minelli director and father of Liza.
May 26 – Bob Hope, English-born US actor, comedian and singer.
June 18 – Jeanette MacDonald, US singer and actress.
September 13 – Claudette Colbert, actress.

Literature

GEORGE ORWELL

Eric Arthur Blair, known later as George Orwell, was born on June 25 in Bengal, India, where his father worked for the Civil Service. At the age of one, he returned to England with his mother and was not to see his father again for three years.

After an education at Eton, he joined the Burmese Police where he stayed for five years, despite his hatred of what he called this 'unsuitable profession'.

In 1928, he left to face 'poverty and a sense of failure', and even endured periods of homelessness, before finding part-time work in a bookshop. He turned his experiences to good use, by describing them in his first books, *Down and Out in Paris and London* (1933) and *The Road to Wigan* (1937). In 1933, he adopted the pen name George Orwell which reflected his love of the English countryside – choosing the Patron Saint of England and his favourite river, which flows through Suffolk.

After fighting in the Spanish Civil War, where Orwell was shot in the neck, he began to write book reviews for *The New English Weekly*. In the Second World War he worked for the BBC, before becoming literary editor of the *Tribune,* and in 1944 his anti-Stalinist novel *Animal Farm* was published to great acclaim. This was followed four years later by the classic *1984*, a bleak futuristic view of a society under a totalitarian state. Several phrases and ideas from this book have now entered the English language, including 'Room 101', 'thought police' and 'Big Brother'.

Orwell was married twice; first for 11 years to Eileen O'Shaunnessy, with whom he adopted a son and, four years after her death, to Sonia Brownell. His second marriage was short-lived – a few months later, in January 1950, he died from tuberculosis.

EVELYN WAUGH

Born Arthur Evelyn St John Waugh, on October 28, in London, his family's literary leaning made it almost inevitable that he would become a writer. His father, Arthur, was a noted editor and publisher and, by the time Evelyn was old enough to go to secondary school, older brother Alec had already published his first novel, *The Loom of Youth,* which was based in the very public school from which he had recently been expelled.

With such novels as *Vile Bodies, Decline and Fall* and *A Handful of Dust*, Evelyn became known as the leading satirical writer of his generation. His novels ridiculed the very circles in which he liked to move – the English upper-class. After a conversion to Catholicism in 1930, religion became a prevalent theme in his books, most notably in the 1945 classic, *Brideshead Revisited*.

Waugh's first marriage, in 1928, was to the Hon. Evelyn Gardner. To avoid confusion, their friends called them He-Evelyn and She-Evelyn! The couple divorced in 1930, and Evelyn married Laura Herbert and went on to have seven children, the second of which, Auberon, became a successful author and journalist. Waugh died of a heart attack in 1966 and is buried in Somerset.

LITERARY WORKS

Henry James' novel, *The Ambassadors*, was serialised in 12 monthly instalments in *North American Review*. The dark comedy follows the fortunes of Lewis Strether, as he travels across Europe in pursuit of his widowed fiancée's wayward son.

Beatrix Potter published *The Tale of Squirrel Nutkin*, and novels included Jack London's *The Call of the Wild* and Samuel Butler's *The Way of all Flesh*.

BIRTHS

February 13 – Georges Simenon, Belgian writer and creator of Maigret.
June 25 – George Orwell, novelist.
July 10 – John Wyndham, British writer.
October 28 – Evelyn Waugh, novelist.

DEATHS

January 22 – Augustus Hare, biographer and travel writer.

Architecture

LIVERPOOL CATHEDRAL

The year-long competition to design Liverpool Cathedral came to a close and 22-year-old Giles Gilbert Scott was announced as the surprise winner. An architectural student, with no buildings to his name, he beat 100 entries, including luminaries such as Charles Rennie Mackintosh and Charles Herbert Reilly. The choice of Scott was even more contentious to followers of the Anglican Church when it emerged he was Roman Catholic.

Because of his inexperience, it was decided that Scott should work under the supervision of established architect George Bodley, but Scott resented his input and the two men never got on. After Bodley's death, Scott decided to revise his original entry and, in 1910, he replaced his two towers with one very tall tower in the centre, topped with a lantern. Much of his original Gothic style was lost and replaced with a more modern, monumental style, making the interior more spacious.

The Cathedral, now one of two in the city, stretches over an area of 9,600 square metres and is built from sandstone, quarried in the suburb of Woolton. The 100-metre belltower remains one of the tallest in the world and houses the highest bells in the world at 66 metres. One of the stained-glass windows depicts Bodley and Scott sitting together.

Art

AN ICONIC IMAGE

A contract with advertising company Brown and Bigelow, of Minesotta, led to artist C.M. Coolidge producing his first *Dogs Playing Poker* picture.

Sixteen oil paintings showing dogs in human pursuits were commissioned as part of a campaign to advertise cigars. Of those, nine show the animals playing poker and were so popular that they inspired a host of imitations and numerous print runs.

At an auction in 2005, two of the originals, *A Bold Bluff* and *Waterloo*, were sold for $590,000 (£290,500) at auction – over ten times the estimate.

New York artist Cassius Marcellus Coolidge is also credited with the invention of 'Comic Foregrounds' – the life-sized cut-outs with holes at head level that you can put your head through to be photographed.

PARISIAN REVOLT

Until 1903, the Parisian art calendar was dominated by the Salon Paris, the official exhibition organised by the Société des Artistes Français. But many great artists felt that the committee's views and choices were too conservative and a splinter group, including Pierre-Auguste Renior and Henri Matisse, decided to set up their own event.

The *Salon d'Automne*, which displayed works by such greats as Matisse, Auguste Rodin, Jacques Villon and Renoir, went from strength to strength during the first half of the Twentieth Century and became a show-piece for innovation.

DEATH OF GAUGUIN

On May 9, French artist Paul Gauguin died on the Marquesas Islands in French Polynesia, where he had made his home.

After stints in the Merchant Marines and the Navy, the young Parisian began his career as a stockbroker and moved to Copenhagen with his Danish wife Mette. In 1883, he gave up his job to become a full-time artist, leaving his wife and five children in Denmark, where poverty meant they had to live with her family, while he returned to Paris.

Hugely influenced by Van Gogh, with whom he spent several months in Arles in 1888, he suffered from bouts of depression and, in 1891, disillusioned and destitute, he left France for Tahiti. There, he frequently clashed with the colonial authorities over their treatment of the natives and in 1903, he was sentenced to three months in prison. He died of syphilis, at the age of 54, before his sentence began.

His style in the latter years of his life was hugely influenced by the primitive culture of the Polynesians and his romanticised view of their lifestyle.

On November 9, 2006, an auction of Twentieth-Century art at Christie's New York saw Gauguin's *Man with an Axe* fetch $40.3m (£21m) – a record for the Post-impressionist.

WHISTLER SILENCED

July 14 saw the death of another great artist, James Abbott McNeill Whistler. The American artist was born in Lowell, Masachussetts, in 1834, although he often claimed to have been born in Russia, where his father worked for a time. 'I shall be born when and where I want, and I do not choose to be born in Lowell,' he famously declared.

At 21 he gave up a military career to travel to Paris and paint, with the Impressionists, before moving to London, where he was to settle.

A famous wit, Whistler became great friends with Oscar Wilde, with whom he socialised in both London and Paris. At one of Whistler's dinner parties, it is said, Wilde heard his host make a biting remark. Wilde apparently said, 'I wish I'd said that', to which the artist replied 'You will, Oscar, you will!' Sadly the men fell out when Wilde was exposed as a homosexual and Whistler openly ridiculed him.

In 1877, a bad review from critic John Ruskin, who accused him of 'flinging a pot of paint in the public's face', led Whistler to sue. The action was successful but the court proceedings were lengthy and expensive and, when damages were set at a mere farthing, he was left bankrupt.

At 54, Whistler married Beatrix, the widow of architect E.W.Godwin, who died five years later of cancer. Whistler died ten years later, at the age of 69, and is buried in Chiswick, London.

Whistler's most famous work is *Arrangement in Gray and Black: Portrait of the Artist's Mother*, which is housed in the Musée d'Orsay in Paris.

FAREWELL TO THE FATHER

In November, Camille Pissarro, the Father of Impressionism, also passed away. Born to French-Jewish parents in the West Indies, his desire to paint inspired him to run away to Venezuela as a young man and, as a result, his parents sent him to Paris to study art. There he met Monet and Corot and became a leading light in the Impressionist movement.

Specialising in landscapes, Pissarro made many trips to London where he painted such views as Dulwich College and Kew Gardens. He also dabbled in pointillism, in which tones are built from tiny dots of pure colour.

His generosity to younger artists, including Gauguin and Paul Cézanne, made him a patriarchal figure in the movement. Of his own eight children, only six survived to adulthood and all were painters, the most successful of whom was Lucien Pissarro.

In 2001, Sotheby's sold Pissarro's Parisian view, *La Rue St. Lazare*, for $6,605,750 (£3.3m), a record for the artist at auction.

THE BIRTH OF A BRITISH LEGEND

On January 10, sculptress Barbara Hepworth was born in Wakefield, Yorkshire. The daughter of a county surveyor, she studied at Leeds College of Art, after which she won a travelling scholarship to Italy, where she learned to carve in stone and married sculptor John Skeaping. In 1928, the couple shared an exhibition at the Beaux Art Gallery in London. A year later their son, Paul, was born.

In 1931 Barbara met painter Ben Nicholson, who was to become her second husband and with whom she developed her abstract style, which was unveiled in exhibitions in the Lefevre Gallery.

Three years later, she gave birth to triplets Simon, Rachel and Sarah and, shortly afterwards, the family moved to Cornwall. In 1949, Barbara bought the Trewyn Studios in St Ives, where she lived and worked until her death, in a fire at the building, at the age of 72.

Barbara's hugely influential work has been exhibited all over the world. Her most famous pieces include *Sphere with Inner Form*, *Figures in a Landscape* and *Winged Figure* – which hangs on the side of John Lewis department store in London's Oxford Street. In 1965, she became Dame Barbara Hepworth when she was awarded a DBE.

BIRTHS

January 10 – Dame Barbara Hepworth, sculptor.
July 21 – Roy Neuberger, art collector and supporter.
August 24 – Graham Sutherland, painter.
December 24 – Joseph Cornell, American sculptor.

DEATHS

May 9 – Paul Gauguin, painter.
July 14 – James McNeill Whistler, American painter and etcher.
September 13 – Carl Schuch, painter.
November 12 – Camille Pissarro, Impressionist painter.

Travel and Transport

FORD MOTOR COMPANY FORMED

Henry Ford launched the Ford Motor Company, with 12 investors, on June 16, 1903.

Encouraged by the success of the popular Oldsmobile, now being produced at the rate of 4,000 a year by the Olds Motor Vehicle Company, Ford launched his company in a factory in Detroit with $28,000 in cash. Amongst the backers were John and Horace Dodge, who had a thriving business making auto-parts at their Dodge Brothers Bicycle & Machine Factory.

The son of a farmer, Ford had worked as a machinist and engineer with the Edison Company and had experimented with automobiles in his spare time. In 1896, he had completed his first car and resigned from the Edison Company to set up the Detroit Automobile Company in 1899. But a disagreement with his associates led to him forming the Ford Motor Company.

In July 1903 the company sold its first production car, a two-cylinder Model A, to Dr. Ernst Pfenning of Chicago.

THE 'FLYER' MAKES AVIATION HISTORY

Wilbur and Orville Wright flew a gasoline-powered airplane over the beach at Kitty Hawk, North Carolina on December 17. It was the first powered, heavier-than-air machine to achieve controlled, sustained flight with a pilot aboard.

The airplane, named *The Flyer*, took off from a launching ramp, with Orville piloting in a harness under the wings. It flew for 12

now small, and it will certainly be lost next year, when further Russian reinforcements arrive.

BALLOONLESS AIRSHIP.

(From Our Own Correspondent.)

NEW YORK, Friday, Dec. 18.

Messrs. Wilbur and Orville Wright, of Ohio, yesterday successfully experimented with a flying machine at Kittyhawk, North Carolina. The machine has no balloon attachment, and derives its force from propellers worked by a small engine.

In the face of a wind blowing twenty-one miles an hour the machine flew three miles at the rate of eight miles an hour, and descended at a point selected in advance. The idea of the box-kite was used in the construction of the airship.

LEGACY OF THREE MILLIONS.

(From Our Own Correspondent.)

VIENNA, Wednesday, Dec. 16.

Lieutenant Barth, an officer belonging to a Hungarian regiment of Hussars stationed at Debreczen, has resigned his commission,

The Wright Brothers made aviation history in The Flyer with their 12 second flight.

seconds and a distance of 120 feet. The airplane was flown three more times that day, with Orville and Wilbur alternating as pilot. The longest flight, with Wilbur at the controls, was 852 feet and lasted 59 seconds.

DRIVING LICENCE INTRODUCED

The Motor Car Act of 1903 required the registration of all motor cars and the licensing of drivers in the UK.

Each car was issued with a unique registration number and fines were introduced for reckless driving. The speed limit was increased from 14 mph to 20 mph.

There was no driving test required, as yet. Car owners paid 20 shillings to register their vehicle and five shillings for a licence.

PARIS METRO FIRE

A fire on the Paris Metro killed 84 people on August 10, most at Couronnes station.

The first sign of trouble was at 6.53 p.m., when a train arrived at Boulevard Barbès station with heavy smoke pouring from the front car.

Angry passengers were evacuated onto the platform and, in order to resume service, the train moved on, but the fire and smoke increased as it proceeded along the track.

The driver of a train behind, packed with passengers, could see the smoke ahead. He stopped at the next station for people to evacuate to the street but by this time the fire was out of control.

Disoriented by the smoke and far from the exit, many people wandered the wrong way until they succumbed to asphyxia or were consumed by the flames.

RECORD TRAIN SPEEDS

Electric trains from Siemens and AEG reached record speeds in Berlin in October. The first, on October 6, notched up 128.4 mph. Two weeks later it was beaten by another that reached 130.7 mph.

Toys

US TOY FAIR

The first Toy Fair in America was held in 1903 by the Toy Fair Chamber of Commerce. The annual event in New York was to become the biggest of its kind.

CRAYOLA CRAYONS INVENTED

The first modern, coloured crayons were invented and mass produced by US chemical company Binney & Smith.

Early crayons were developed in Europe and probably consisted of a mixture of charcoal and oil. Later, wax was substituted for the oil.

In the early 1900s cousins, Edwin Binney and C. Harold Smith, began to produce slate pencils and a type of dustless chalk for the educational market. They realised that a new wax crayon they had developed to mark crates and boxes in their factory would provide a neater and more affordable alternative to costly, imported crayons for American schools.

They refined the crayons, making them non-toxic and were able to create eight colours for them – black, blue, brown, green, orange, red, violet, and yellow.

The brand name Crayola was picked by Edwin Binney's wife, Alice. She attached the French word for chalk, craie, with 'ola,' from oleaginous or oily.

In 1903 they started to mass-produce the crayons and sold them in packets of eight to a delighted American public.

TEDDY BEAR MANIA

Soft and jointed toy bears, also known as 'Teddy Bears', made by German toy manufacturer Steiff, were shown at the Leipzig Trade Fair in Germany in March. They were a big hit and resulted in an American buyer placing an order for 3,100 bears. By the end of that year, the order had increased to 13,000 and, by 1907, the Steiff Company was selling over 1,000,000 bears.

Sport

TOUR DE FRANCE BEGINS

In Paris a new bicycle race was announced for 1903 called the Tour de France.

The idea for an around-France stage race came from the chief cycling journalist of the newspaper *L'Auto*, 26-year-old Géo Lefèvre.

The newspaper announced this exciting but gruelling race on January 19, 1903. There were six stages and no convenient breaks for sleep but the prize money was 20,000 francs. Competitors were expected to ride through the night. Sixty cyclists took part in the event, which began on July 1 and ended 19 days later. They travelled 2,500 kilometres.

Only 20 of the riders finished the race, which was won by Maurice Garin with a time of 94 hours 33 minutes and 14 seconds.

BIGGEST FA CUP FINAL WIN

The 1903 FA Cup Final between Bury and Derby County at Crystal Palace was a one sided affair with Bury winning 6–0. Goals came from George Ross, Charles Sagar, Joe Leeming (2), William Wood and John Plant. The game has entered the record books as the biggest-ever win in an FA Cup Final.

FOSTER IN TIP TOP FORM

England batsman R.E 'Tip' Foster, the Worcestershire amateur, made a sensational start to his international cricket career. He scored 287 for England against Australia in Sydney, on December 14, which was then the highest individual score ever made in a test match.

Reginald Erskine 'Tip' Foster was an accomplished sportsman who also played football for England and is the only man to have captained England at both sports simultaneously.

He was educated at Malvern College and University College, Oxford, one of seven brothers who all played for Malvern and Worcestershire.

Tip and his brother W.L. Foster set a unique record of both scoring a century for Worcestershire in a match against Hampshire. In 1900 he set the record for the highest individual score in the Varsity Match and scored two hundred for the Gentlemen against the Players at Lord's. For these performances, he was named Wisden Cricketer of the Year in 1901.

In football, he was a forward for Corinthians in the early 1900s and played six times for England between 1900 and 1902. He was awarded the captaincy against Wales in his final appearance on 3 March 1902.

The Home

The problem of overcrowding in cities had already led to the building of such estates as Bournville and Port Sunlight, founded by the Cadbury brothers and soap magnate William Heskith Lever respectively. These were designed for workers in specific factories and were laid out like the traditional English village. In 1903, Britain entered a new phase in housing with the building of Letchworth, the first Garden City.

The 'Garden City' was the brainchild of reformer Ebenezer Howard who published plans in his 1898 book *Tomorrow* and again in his 1902 *Garden Cities of Tomorrow.* He argued that workers should not be crammed together in towns, or forced to travel long distances from the suburbs. A Garden City would contain shops and factories but be small enough for a good social network.

Howard recommended that the town contained no more than 30,000 inhabitants, with around 2000 more living on farms in surrounding rural areas, and that residents could benefit from plenty of open space and fresh air.

The Garden City should combine 'the most energetic and active town life with all the beauty and delight of the country'. He urged planners to take advantage of the fact that there were few existing buildings in the area 'by so laying out a Garden City that, as it grows, the free gifts of nature – fresh air, sunlight, breathing space, playing room – shall be retained in all needed abundance . . . and life become an abiding joy and delight'.

In Letchworth, no more than 12 houses were permitted in each acre, which were set in tree-lined roads with plenty of playing fields and open spaces. By 1914, 9,000 people had settled there and the success of the project meant that other architects laid out their estates in a more spacious design. Howard's ideas also spawned the now familiar phrase 'town planning'.

Welwyn Garden City was built along the same lines in 1919.

The Changing Role of Women

The peaceful approach of Millicent Fawcett and her National Union of Women's Suffrage frustrated the more militant advocates for voting rights and, on October 10, some decided to go a step further.

An historic meeting in a house in Nelson Street, Manchester, saw six women, including Emmeline Pankhurst and her daughter Christabel, form a new alliance which they called the Women's Social and Political Union. Membership was limited to women only and the motto, *Deeds not Words,* was a portent for the direct action to come.

Emmeline Pankhurst, who quickly emerged as the leader of the new group, summed up their beliefs in the following statement:

> *'If civilization is to advance at all in the future, it must be through the help of women, women freed of their political shackles, women with full power to work their will in society.'*

Previous suffragists had sought to groom Members of Parliament to defend their cause but had been constantly held back by the refusal of Parliament even to debate the subject.

Although they were not dubbed 'Suffragettes' until 1906, when a *Daily Mail* journalist coined the phrase as an insult, these women had plans that would radically change the face of female emancipation. For the next few years the group's activities would involve hunger strikes, demonstrations and, a decade on, the death of Emily Davison under the hooves of the King's horse.

FIRST FEMALE NEWSPAPER EDITOR

As the Pankhursts were making history in Manchester, young female journalist Mary Howarth became the first editor of a new publication entitled The *Daily Mirror.* The paper was established by Alfred Harmsworth, who believed that the popularity of the women's section in his hugely successful *Daily Mail* indicated that there was a market for a daily for 'gentlewomen'.

Promoting Mary from this section to run her own ship, he ploughed £100,000 into the launch and was rewarded with initial sales of 276,000. However, the circulation plummeted to 24,801 by January 1904, when the paper was losing £3,000 a week.

Mary's trailblazing new job didn't last long. She was replaced by Hamilton Fyfe and the *Daily Mirror* was transformed into a tabloid for men.

MARTHA WASHINGTON HOTEL

On March 2, the first hotel exclusively for women was opened in New York. The 12-storey boarding house was named after the original First Lady and had rooms for 600 guests.

'The hotel is expected to appeal chiefly to women who earn their own living,' said a contemporary article in the *Herald Tribune*. 'There are four hundred single rooms and suites to be let by the week at rates ranging from $3 to $17, and about two hundred rooms will be at the disposal of transients.'

The Martha Washington Hotel operated as a women-only establishment until 1998 when a property developer who had bought the business changed the historic policy and allowed men through the hallowed doors.

Science

REVOLUTIONARY EYE OP

Lieutenant-Colonel Henry Smith of the Indian Medical Service began conducting a new operation for cataracts. He produced good vision in 99.4 per cent of the 1,023 operations performed in the first four months of the year by extracting the capsule containing the opaque lens.

Colonel Smith was an Irish-born British surgeon assigned primarily to the hospital in Jullundur, Punjab, India, where he was a civil medical officer and rapidly established a reputation in general surgery.

However, from his early days at Jullundur in the early 1890s, he devoted his attention to eye diseases and eye surgery.

He had remarkable success with his method of extraction of the cataract within the capsule and became one of the major figures in the history of cataract surgery. An unusual part of his procedure was to smoke a cigar whilst operating! When asked about the danger this might cause to his patients, Colonel Smith replied, 'There is nothing as sterile as cigar ashes!'

MARCONI'S WIRELESS TELEGRAPHY

US President Theodore Roosevelt sent a message of greetings to King Edward VII using Guglielmo Marconi's wireless radio transmission.

Italian inventor Marconi had made a few earlier transmissions across a much shorter expanse but this one, across the Atlantic on January 18, launched the era of global wireless communications.

Standing at his radio station in Wellfleet, Massachusetts, Marconi tapped out the President's message in Morse code, which was relayed through Nova Scotia and on to another station at the southern tip of Cornwall via radio waves. A few hours later, he received the King's reply.

In March, a regular news service between London and New York began, using Marconi's wireless.

ELECTROCARDIOGRAM DEMONSTRATED

In Holland on November 3, Willem Einthoven demonstrated his new invention for monitoring the heart – an electrocardiograph. It worked by recording the electrical activity of the heat. Einthoven was to receive a Nobel Prize in Medicine for his invention in 1924.

Chapter Five

1904

Politics

THE ENTENTE CORDIALE

BRITAIN AND France settled years of dispute and conflict with the signing of the Entente Cordiale, on April 8.

The historic agreement came at a time when Britain had lost confidence after the early humiliations experienced in the Boer War, and felt a growing unease about an aggressive Germany.

With the outbreak of the Russo-Japanese War, France and Britain found themselves on the point of being dragged into the conflict on the side of their respective allies – France with Russia and Britain with Japan. In order to avoid this, they shook off ancient rivalry and united to resolve colonial differences in Africa, America, Asia and the Pacific.

The Entente was composed of three documents. The first and most important document was the declaration concerning Egypt and Morocco. France was allowed to preserve order and provide assistance in Morocco, whilst Britain would have primacy in Egypt.

The second document dealt with a fishing rights dispute going back centuries. France agreed to give up shore rights along the western coast. In return, Britain made small territorial concessions to France in West Africa.

The final declaration concerned various territorial disputes in Siam (Thailand), Madagascar and the New Hebrides.

The agreement capped months of delicate negotiations. The initiative for the conference came from King Edward VII when he visited Paris the previous year.

Royalty

OPEN PARKLAND AND CLEAN WATER

Many more people were to enjoy the benefits of beautiful parkland and clean water this year. On March 29, King Edward VII opened Richmond Royal Park to the public. And on July 21, he and Queen Alexandra travelled to Powys, Wales, to open the Elan Valley dams and reservoirs.

Work on this ambitious civil engineering project had begun in 1893 and was not fully completed until 1906. The royal party boarded a special train running on the Elan railway at Rhayader station and travelled west along the valley with the trackside lined with soldiers in their best uniforms. The King, using an ornate handwheel, turned on the new supply at the filter beds near Elan Village to send a flow of clean water on its way to Birmingham along the 73-mile aqueduct.

Historical Events

DEATH OF EXPLORER STANLEY

Sir Henry Morton Stanley, who became the most famous explorer of his time, died in London on May 10, aged 63. He became famous for his epic 1,500 mile search for Dr David Livingstone in Central Africa in 1871.

Born in Denbigh, Wales on January 28, 1841, he went to America in 1859 and served on both sides in the American Civil War before working as a sailor and a journalist.

In 1869, he was sent by the *New York Herald* to Africa in search of Scottish missionary and explorer David Livingstone, of whom little had been heard since 1866 when he had set off to find the source of the Nile.

Stanley found the sick explorer on November 10, 1871, in Ujiji, near Lake Tanganyika in present-day Tanzania, and greeted him with the now famous, 'Dr. Livingstone, I presume?'

When Livingstone died in 1873, Stanley resolved to continue his exploration of the region. In 1890, he returned to Britain, married, and began a worldwide lecture tour. He became MP for Lambeth in South London, serving from 1895 to 1900, and was knighted in 1899.

JAPAN DECLARES WAR ON RUSSIA

A surprise night raid by Japanese torpedo boats on the Russian fleet at Port Arthur on February 10, plunged the two countries into war.

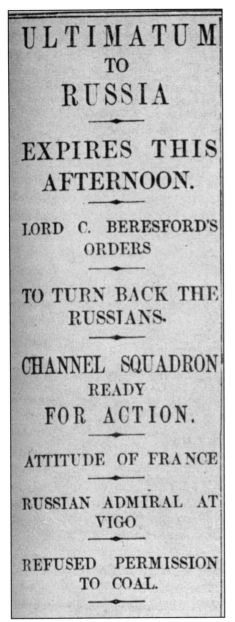

ULTIMATUM TO RUSSIA

EXPIRES THIS AFTERNOON.

LORD C. BERESFORD'S ORDERS

TO TURN BACK THE RUSSIANS.

CHANNEL SQUADRON

READY

FOR ACTION.

ATTITUDE OF FRANCE

RUSSIAN ADMIRAL AT VIGO

REFUSED PERMISSION TO COAL.

Britain became caught up in the war between Japan and Russia in October when the Russian Baltic fleet fired on British fishing trawlers near Hull, believing them to be Japanese torpedo boats. Russia and Britain were on the brink of but a half-hearted apology from the Russian squadron commander, Admiral Rozhestvensky calmed the situation - that and Lord Beresford' Channel Fleet following the Russians for three days to ensure no further problems.

Tension had been building between the two countries over imperialist interests in Manchuria and Korea.

On February 1, Britain and France agreed to remain neutral in event of a war. Three days later, the Tsar, in an attempt to avert hostilities, offered Japan a free hand in Korea if Japan left Manchuria to the Russians.

The Japanese followed their attack by sending 8,000 infantry on their way to Seoul, capital of Korea.

Fierce fighting continued throughout the year with heavy losses on both sides but with Japan consistently getting the better of their enemy. Japanese dominance surprised world leaders who were forced to view them as a serious emerging global power.

The embarrassing string of defeats further increased the Russian people's dissatisfaction with the Tsar, whom they considered to be inefficient and corrupt.

Social Change

NO SMOKING PLEASE

An investigation carried out by the Meteorological Council had concluded, in 1903, that 20 per cent of London fogs were caused by smoke and that the density and duration of every 'smog' was increased by smoke.

On March 22, 1904, the Coal Smoke Abatement Society held its fifth annual meeting where it called for a smokeless capital.

British Industry was largely to blame, with more than 50,000 coal-powered steam engines belching out enormous quantities of black smoke. But homeowners also contributed, as their houses were heated with coal fires.

One particular homeowner was singled out for criticism by the chairman of the Coal Smoke Abatement Society, who told a Royal Commission, 'Upon my word the Duke of Wellington's house is like a factory chimney in the morning. In fact, some of the factories do not emit so much smoke as the Duke of Wellington's house.'

One answer to the problem came with the invention of the smokeless fuel Coalite, by engineer Thomas Parker.

Proof that smoking can kill was seen with the dramatic death of leading financier, Whitaker Wright, the 'man of millions' who, losing a case of fraud, was sentenced to seven years. As he stepped down from the dock, he lit a cigar and promptly fell down dead, poisoned by the prussic Acid he'd just administered to himself in the cigar. His estate was sold by the state and locals bought Hindhead Common which they donated to the National Trust.

RELIEF FOR THE POOR

Figures released in November showed a huge increase in the poor relief handed out by charities. Almost 800,000 people in England and Wales received help, equating to one person in every 41. Of these, 122,000 lived in London.

A quarter of a million people were forced to live in workhouses. The eastern counties, such as Suffolk, Essex and Norfolk, were reported to be worst affected.

In Scotland, the Departmental Committee on Poor Law Medical Relief and the Rules and Regulations for the Management of Poor Houses reported an improvement in conditions in the larger poorhouse hospitals, but recommended that the sick should always be in a building separate from the rest of the poorhouse and that nursing by paupers should be abolished.

HEALTH AND EDUCATION

The Interdepartmental Committee on Physical Deterioration published a report on various health matters and made recommendations to be implemented over 50 years.

Among the ideas was the appointment of medical officers in highly populated areas and of health visitors in every area. Still births were to be registered and laws against smoke pollution were to be enforced.

Corporal punishment were an accepted part of everyday school life but the provisions of school meals and free medical examination, plus health education for schoolchildren were an advance in the education system. This delightful postcard from 1904 is one of many collectable Edwardian postcards, many of them affordable – expect to pay £5-10 for a similar one.

At school, children were to receive free medical examinations, and there was to be the provision of school meals and classes in health education, including instruction about the effects of alcohol.

Elsewhere in education, the system of 'payment by results', whereby the government grant to a school was determined by the attendance and exam results of the pupils, was abolished.

POSTCARDS

A craze for postcards took over British mail rooms. The Postmaster-General's report showed that the volume of cards sent in the previous year had increased by 25 percent, and by 35 percent in Scotland.

The trend for postcards had started on the continent but had quickly

Postcards were a very popular form of communication with the messages as brief as modern texts. Many people simply wrote that they'd arrived home safely or thanked their recipients for a pleasant day out in an age where courtesy was very important. This is part of a series of innocent children, carefully coloured. Another affordable postcard, expect to pay £5-8.

taken off in the UK, where scenes depicted anything from a royal event or the portrait of an actress to a popular advertisement of the day. Unlike today's use as holiday missives, many people bought them as souvenirs or used them to send short messages. With seven postal deliveries a day, it was a quick and reliable way to keep in touch, and millions passed through the postal system every week.

However, according to the Postmaster-General's report, the humble letter was still the dominant way of communicating, with 2,597,600,000 delivered compared to 613,000,000 postcards.

Today, Edwardian postcards have become popular collectables and rare designs are sold for hundreds of pounds at auction.

Edward VII, when Prince of Wales, had sparked an interest in the sailor suit as a fashionable item. Still in vogue, this advert shows just how stylish it could be, here topped with a newly designed yachting cap for ladies.

This is the Capeline Ombrella, or Umbrella Hat, the Lace Fall of which is intended to Shade the Eyes and Obviate the Use of a Parasol.

New century fashions

Fashion was often very practical, such as this advert from *The Daily Mail* for the Umbrella Hat.

Fashion

WEATHER GIRLS

Advances in travel and transport also brought about a fashion revolution in weatherproofing. Aquascutum and Burberry were two of the companies who specialised in outdoor clothing for field sports and motoring, Burberry even developed a range for polar expeditions, ballooning and aviation.

In 1904 the company was producing a full ladies' range, including 'Skirt Sacs' for motoring, which 'envelope the lady's skirt in a rug formed like a sac and fitted with a rubber foot board with a camel fleece lining'. They also produced a golfing suit with pivot sleeves for 'perfect arm swing' and a women's 'weatherall' – 'useful for coaching, yachting and racing'. Motoring veils, tied at the neck to keep the dust off the face and hair, were also popular.

THE GIBSON GIRL IN LONDON

At the beginning of the new century, the so-called 'Gibson Girl' had become the beauty standard for women everywhere. Based on the popular pictures and postcards by Charles Dana Gibson, the original was inspired by the three Langhorne sisters – one of whom, Irene, was married to the artist.

The Gibson girl had an hour-glass figure, long legs, ample chest and a slim neck. She was beautiful and stylish, with the classic S-shaped corset and hair piled onto her head in the fashionable bouffant style.

Named after the artist, Charles Dana Gibson's art and postcards and based on his wife and her sisters, the three Langhorne sisters, the Gibson Girl was the epitome of beauty and elegance.

In 1904, American actress Camille Clifford, who had recently won $2,000 (£1,000) in a magazine competition – sponsored by Gibson – to find the human epitome of his illustrated beauty, came to London. Already synonymous with the character on the American stage, Camille's amazing figure and legendary beauty caused a sensation when she appeared at the Shaftesbury Theatre.

In France, Italian-born fashion designer Maria Nielli, known as Nina, married jeweller Luigi Ricci. Her hugely successful fashion house would not be set up until 1932, when Madame Ricci was 50.

Entertainment

FILM

Georges Méliès stunned audiences once more with his silent film *The Impossible Voyage*. The innovative director, who had pioneered special effects in *Le Voyage dans la Lune* (*The Trip to the Moon*) two years earlier, based his latest film on Jules Verne's play *Voyage à travers l'impossible*. It tells the story of an ambitious geographic society which travels round the world using a car, a train and a submarine. With balloons attached to their train, they travel up the Swiss Alps and are lifted out of the earth's atmosphere to land on the sun.

Not only was the trick photography incredible for the era but the film ran at a full 20 minutes, five times longer than the usual films of the age.

Although cinema was still in its infancy, remakes were already on the agenda. One of the films released, *The Great Train Robbery*, was a rehash of the classic from 1903.

On April 14, in the Fulham Theatre, audiences experienced the first attempt at 'talking pictures', using the phonograph to produce sound to accompany the film.

THEATRE

J.M. Barrie's most famous character, *Peter Pan*, came to life at the Duke of York Theatre in London on December 27. The play, which starred Nina Boucicault as Peter and Gerald du Maurier as Captain Hook, was praised by audiences and critics and became the hit of the season.

The story of *Peter Pan* or *The Boy Who Wouldn't Grow Up* was hugely influenced by Barrie's friendship with Sylvia Llewelyn Davies and her five boys, George, John, Peter, Michael and Nicholas.

It is also thought that the tragic death of Barrie's brother David, shortly before his fourteenth birthday, contributed to the idea. Barrie's mother, who never got over David's death and distanced herself from young James, was said to take comfort in the fact that her beloved son would remain a boy forever. In 1911, J.M. Barrie adapted the story into a book, entitled *Peter Pan and Wendy* and in 1929 he gave the copyright to Great Ormond Street Hospital.

Also in London, the Coliseum theatre opened in St. Martin's Lane on Christmas Eve. The impressive building was designed by Frank Matcham, the architect behind the Palladium, for impresario Oswald Stoll, and was intended to be the largest 'people's palace of entertainment' in the country. The opening night was devoted to an evening of variety acts.

MUSIC

Enrico Caruso proved a huge hit with an American audience when he appeared in *L'Elisir d'Amore* at the New York Metropolitan Opera, shortly after making his first American recording – *La Donna é Mobile.*

On February 17, Puccini's *Madame Butterfly* opened at La Scala in Milan but was universally panned. By May, the opera had been revised by splitting the overlong second act into two and changing some of the scenes. The new version was a huge success when staged at the Italian city of Brescia and it later transferred to New York.

Popular hits of the year included *Give my Regards to Broadway* by George M.Cohan and *Meet me in St. Louis, Louis* by Andrew B. Sterling and Kerry Mills.

BIRTHS

January 18 – Cary Grant, British actor.
February 29 – Jimmy Dorsey, US bandleader.
March 1 – Glenn Miller, US bandleader.
April 14 – John Gielgud, British actor.
May 2 – Bing Crosby, US singer and actor.
May 21 – Fats Waller, US jazz musician.
May 26 – George Formby, British actor, singer, variety act.
June 2 –Johnny Weissmuller, US swimmer and Tarzan star.
June 26 – Peter Lorre, German actor.
August 21 – Count Basie, US jazz musician.
September 29 – Greer Garson, US actress.
October 20 – Anna Neagle, British actress.

DEATHS

May 1 – Antonín Dvorak, composer.

Literature

Published in *The Strand Magazine*, Arthur Conan Doyle's famous detective was back in *The Return of Sherlock Holmes* in 1903. Serialised until December 1904, these images are from the 10th story in the series, *The Adventure of the Golden Pince-Nez*, illustrated by Sidney Paget.

THE STRAND MAGAZINE.

Vol. xxviii.   JULY, 1904.   No. 163.

THE RETURN OF
SHERLOCK HOLMES.

By A. CONAN DOYLE.

X.—*The Adventure of the Golden Pince-Nez.*

HEN I look at the three massive manuscript volumes which contain our work for the year 1894 I confess that it is very difficult for me, out of such a wealth of material, against the windows. It was strange there in the very depths of the town, with ten miles of man's handiwork on every side of us, to feel the iron grip of Nature, and to be conscious that to the huge elemental forces all London was no more than the molehills

PULITZER'S LEGACY

Writing his will seven years before his death, journalist and publisher Joseph Pulitzer made provision for the establishment of the Pulitzer Prize, to be awarded for excellence in various categories of writing. There were to be four awards in journalism, four in letters and drama, one in education and four scholarships.

The Hungarian-born newspaper man was a passionate supporter of America, his adopted homeland, and decided that the literature prizes were to go to an American novel, an original American play performed in New York, a book on the history of the United States, an American biography, and a history of public service by the press.

He also made provisions for a board to oversee the awards after his death and to change them if necessary. The advisory panel, he decreed, was to have the 'power in its discretion to suspend or to change any subject or subjects, substituting, however, others in their places, if in the judgment of the board such suspension, changes, or substitutions shall be conducive to the public good or rendered advisable by public necessities, or by reason of change of time'. The first prizes were awarded in 1917 and, since then, the board has added poetry, music and photography to the list.

CHEKHOV CHECKS OUT

July saw the death of Anton Chekhov, months after completing his classic stage play *The Cherry Orchard*. The grocer's son from Taganrog, Russia, was a doctor by profession and wrote short stories and plays in his spare time. 'Medicine is my lawful wife and literature is my mistress,' he once declared. His initial efforts were poorly received, however, and in 1896 he renounced

Beatrix Potter's tam o'shanter-wearing Benjamin Bunny was first seen in 1904 and has spawned a whole host of collectables, including this figure by Beswick and *(overleaf)* the plate by Royal Albert.

the theatre after the failure of *The Seagull*. A year later the play was revived to great acclaim at the Moscow Arts Theatre and Chekhov's subsequent plays, *Uncle Vanya, Three Sisters* and *The Cherry Orchard* were also premiered there. On July 15, at the age of 44, Chekhov died from tuberculosis at a health spa in Badenweiler, Germany.

Among the books published in 1904 were Frank L. Baum's *The Marvelous Land of Oz*, Henry James' *The Golden Bowl* and Beatrix Potter's *The Tale of Benjamin Bunny*.

BIRTHS

April 27 – Cecil Day-Lewis, Poet Laureate.
Oct 2 – Graham Greene, novelist.
Nov 28 – Nancy Mitford, novelist and biographer.

Architecture

PUTTING UP THE RITZ

Construction began on one of London's most famous hotels, sited on the fashionable street of Piccadilly. The Ritz Hotel was designed by Charles Mewés, architect of the original hotel in Paris, and British designer Arthur Davis, in collaboration with Swedish engineer Sven Bylander. It was the first building in the capital to be built around a steel frame rather than a timber one and was set out to resemble a luxurious French Chateau.

The interior of the seven-storey building was to be completed in the Louis XVI style, with a central Palm Court where refreshments would be served around a gilded fountain. The hotel itself, owned by Swiss hotelier César Ritz, opened in May 1906.

CATHEDRAL GETS UNDERWAY

On July 19, King Edward VII laid the foundation stone for the new cathedral in Liverpool. The building, designed by unknown competition winner Giles Gilbert Scott, was consecrated in 1924 when the altar was finished but was not to open for regular services until 1940. Scott was never to see his masterpiece fully completed as work continued until 1978, a full 75 years after the design was approved and 18 years after the architect's death. He is buried under the building's bell tower.

INNOVATION IN BUFFALO

Frank Lloyd Wright designed a five-storey, red-brick building for the Larkin Soap Company in Buffalo, New York. The building itself was demolished in 1950 but was the very model of innovation in 1904, with plate glass windows, steel desks and suspended toilet bowls. It was also the first fully air-conditioned building on record. 'Nearly every technological innovation used today was suggested in the Larkin Building in 1904,' Wright later claimed.

DEATHS

October 4 – Frédéric Auguste Bartholdi, French sculpture and designer of the Statue of Liberty.

Art

THE WORLD FAIR

On April 30, the Louisiana Purchase Exposition, also known as the World Fair, opened in St Louis to a crowd of 200,000. The event, to commemorate the centenary of a purchase of a huge swathe of land from the French, was opened by the President of the Louisiana Purchase Exposition Company with the words, 'Open ye gates. Swing wide ye Portals.'

Crowds were amazed to see a woodland park transformed by the construction of 1,500 new buildings, including several 'palaces' housing arts, science exhibitions and demonstrations of human progress from the previous century.

One of the most impressive and expensive structures was the Palace of Fine Arts, designed by Cass Gilbert. Made of steel and stone, unlike the timber-framed buildings in the rest of the park, it cost over $1 million and

Meet me in St Louis! Immortalised by the 1944 Vincente Minnelli-Judy Garland film, The Louisiana Purchase Exposition, is better known as the World Fair and attracted 20 million visitors in its seven months. *(Image courtesy of the Estate of Stanley Shoop)*.

108

was intended as a lasting reminder of the fair. Inside, visitors could see paintings, engravings, sculptures and jewellery from artists around the world. The last surviving structure from the event, it is now home to the St Louis Arts Museum.

The centrepiece of the exposition, however, was the Festival Hall. An impressive structure with a seating capacity of 3,500, it stood in the centre of 14 colonnades, representing the 13 states and the Indian territory that were carved out of the Louisiana Purchase. In front of the building, the stunning cascades poured 45,000 gallons of water, per minute, into the Grand Basin.

On the carnival side of the event, a mile-long arcade known as 'The Pike' provided entertainment, with contortionists, dancing girls and animal acts, including *Jim Key the Educated Horse*. There was also the Observation Wheel, which allowed visitors to view the fair from 265 feet in the air.

The World Fair was a huge success. By the time it closed seven months on, an estimated 20 million people had passed through its massive gates.

THE COVERT KISS

A copy of Rodin's *The Kiss* arrived in Lewes, Sussex, four years after it was commissioned by art collector Edward Perry Warren. The eccentric American, who had paid 20,000 Francs for the work, had specified that the male figure's genitals 'must be complete'. In his 1900 letter he had explained that 'being a pagan and lover of antiquities', he wanted the genitals of the man to be sculpted in the classical Greek tradition rather than discreetly hidden.

Curiously, when the sculpture finally arrived, Warren hid it in a stable block for a decade. It is not known whether he was disappointed by the work or whether the size meant he had nowhere else to put it. In 1914, it was lent to Lewes Town Council and displayed in the Town Hall. However, the erotic nature of the piece caused much controversy and in 1917, it returned to its stable home.

The sculpture now belongs to the Tate Modern although, in September 2007, it moved to the Tate Liverpool for the city's eighth centenary celebrations.

CASSATT HONOURED

American impressionist Mary Cassatt was awarded the Légion d'Honneur by the French government for her services to the arts. Although born in

Pennsylvania, Mary spent most of her adult life in France where she was close friends with Edgar Degas. Her work, which often portrayed women with their children, has sold for as much as £1.4 million ($2.8 million) in recent years.

BIRTHS

January 14 – Cecil Beaton, photographer and designer.
May 11 – Salvador Dali, Spanish painter.
April 24 – Willem de Kooning, Dutch painter.

Travel and Transport

LAND SPEED RECORDS SOAR

Henry Ford set a new land speed record of 91.37 mph in his Ford Arrow motor car '999' on frozen Lake St Clair, Michigan, on January 12. The astute businessman knew that such an achievement, with attendant publicity, would result in the sale of more of his cars. However he did admit afterwards that it had scared him so much that he never again wanted to climb into a racing car!

Two weeks later, motor racing and yachting enthusiast. William K. Vanderbilt set a new speed record. Born to a life of luxury, Willie, as he was known, was raised in Vanderbilt mansions, travelled to Europe frequently, and sailed the globe on yachts owned by his millionaire father, who shared the same name.

Willie set a new land speed record of 92.30 mph in a Mercedes at the Daytona Beach Road Course at Ormond Beach, Florida. That same year, he launched the Vanderbilt Cup, the first major trophy in American motor racing. An international event, designed to spur American manufacturers into racing, the race's large cash prize drew from across the Atlantic Ocean the top drivers and their vehicles who had competed in Europe's Gordon Bennett Cup. Held at a course set out in Nassau County on Long Island, New York, the race drew large crowds hoping to see an American car defeat the mighty European vehicles. However, a French Panhard vehicle won the race and fans would have to wait until 1908 when 23-year old George Robertson of Garden City, New York, became the first American to win the Vanderbilt Cup.

The 100 mph barrier was broken on July 21 when Louis Emile Rigolly of France notched up 103.55 mph.

HORSE POWER DOMINATES LONDON

Away from the dazzling land speed records going on in Europe and America, every-day transport in London continued at a sedate pace. In 1904, there were just two motor taxis in the capital amongst 11,000 horse-drawn hansom cabs.

MR ROLLS MEETS MR ROYCE

The Hon. Charles Rolls, whose London company C.S. Rolls sold and repaired cars, and Henry Royce, of Manchester electrical engineers F.H. Royce, had an historic meeting at the Midland Hotel, Manchester, on May 4.

They agreed that Rolls would sell Royce cars under the name 'Rolls-Royce'. Rolls, the third son of Lord Llangattock, was a keen racer from a privileged upbringing. Royce, on the other hand, was a miller's son and a self-made millionaire who established a reputation for perfectionism in engineering.

Their first car, a 10hp two-cylinder model, was exhibited at the Paris Motor Salon in the same year, along with 15hp, 20hp and 30hp models. They were praised for their smooth running and craftsmanship.

TRANS-SIBERIAN RAILWAY

The long-awaited Trans-Siberian Railway – stretching 4,607 miles from Chelyabinsk to Vladivostock – was completed after 13 years of construction, on July 21.

The network of railways connected Moscow and European Russia with the Russian Far East provinces, Mongolia, China and the Sea of Japan. It represented a landmark in railroad engineering. The Russians had to overcome massive problems, including wide rivers and steep gradients around Lake Baikal, permafrost in Eastern Siberia and extremes of temperatures.

With more than 1,000 stations along the route of the railway, the Russian government saw the new railway as a valuable asset in 'opening up' Siberia and promoting trade with China and the Orient.

BROTHERS GET IT WRIGHT

On September 20, the Wright brothers won over sceptics who doubted that their aircraft could actually fly. They had only received limited recognition in 1903 when they made their first flight from Kitty Hawk. So, in May 1904, they invited reporters to watch them take to the air in their new aircraft, Flyer II. But it was a disaster. Engine troubles and slack winds prevented any flying, and they could manage only a very short hops.

Unquestionable success finally came on September 20, 1904, when Wilbur flew the first complete circle by a manned heavier-than-air powered machine, covering 4,080 feet in about a minute and a half.

NEW YORK UNDERGROUND

The New York underground railway opened on October 27 and 150,000 excited passengers used it on its first day.

Toys

MISS MAGIE'S MONOPOLY

As a protest against increases in land values and the capitalist system, Elizabeth Magie, a Quaker from Virginia, came up with *The Landlord's Game*. The game quickly spread through the American Quaker communities and, on its way, the name was changed to *Auction Monopoly* and then simply *Monopoly*, under which title it gained worldwide popularity.

Pennsylvanian Charles Darrow produced the first commercial version in 1934, although there were several attempts to cash in on Magie's idea during the 30 years between.

In the 1920s, Dan Layman came up with a version while playing the game at college, and named it *The Fascinating Game of Finance* after being advised that *Monopoly* was already attached to the earlier idea. In 1930, Ruth Hoskins, the friend of a friend of Layman, claimed to have made her own version, using street names from Atlantic City. Finally, in 1931, Louis Thun, who had explained the rules to his college room-mate Layman in the first place, attempted to patent the board game but had to withdraw the application after a 1904 patent was discovered. Instead Thun gained a copyright on some of the now familiar rules, including the 'community chest' and the $50 'get out of jail' fine.

Out-of-work salesman Charles Darrow eventually sold his version to Parker Brothers in 1935. It became the biggest selling board game of the year and made him the world's first millionaire games designer.

OHIO BUSINESSMAN LOSES HIS MARBLES

The American Marble and Toy Manufacturing Co, the largest toy company in the US in the 1890s, ceased trading due to a devastating fire. Sam Dyke had started his business manufacturing clay marbles in 1884 and, by 1890, had been producing a million a day. When his brother A.L.Dyke set up a rival business in the town, where several others already existed, Sam branched out and his factory produced the first glass marbles in America.

After the factory, which boasted 175 workers and eight furnaces, burned to the ground, children swarmed to the site and gathered up thousands of marbles before the authorities ordered the building's remains to be buried for safety reasons – along with around 10 million marbles.

Today, the site has been transformed into a park but also houses the American Toy Marble Museum.

ROYAL CROWN DERBY

Porcelain manufacturer Royal Crown Derby briefly produced miniature pieces which were used as children's tea-sets and doll's house furniture. The company, which had been appointed to Queen Victoria in 1990, produced tiny copies of tableware, flat irons on stands and coal scuttles, but they were really only intended for display purposes. As so few were made, these miniatures have now become highly collectable.

Sport

THE BIZARRE OLYMPICS

The third modern Olympic Games took place amidst the same apathy of the one in 1900, which was overshadowed by the Paris Exhibition. This time it was reduced to a side-show in St Louis as part of the World Fair.

America won most of the events, since few Europeans turned up because the athletes had to raise the cost of getting there themselves. But the Games were certainly colourful, with bizarre events such as barrel-jumping taking place.

Gold, silver and bronze medals were introduced for the first time. American gymnast George Eyser won six medals even though his left leg was made of wood!

The first man to cross the line in the marathon was New Yorker Fred

Lorz. The crowd cheered him on as he entered the stadium and President Roosevelt's daughter Alice placed a laurel wreath over his head. But just as he was about to receive his medal, officials learned that he had taken a lift half way around in a lorry!

British-born Thomas Hicks, who ran for the American team, was eventually awarded the winner's medal in the marathon. By the end of the race, the exhausted Hicks had to be supported by two of his trainers so that he could cross the finish line.

The Home

ROWNTREE'S SWEET HOUSING PLANS

In response to his son Seebohm's 1901 report into the appalling housing conditions in York, confectionery magnate Joseph Rowntree set up a trust for the building and management of New Earswick. The model village was intended to alleviate the problems of the working classes by offering decent housing, green spaces and community spirit; it was to be built on 150 acres purchased two year earlier, just outside York.

Planners Raymond Unwin and architect Barry Parker, who were also responsible for Letchworth Garden City, worked on the project – which would see 229 houses built over the next 15 years. They were to be open to all low-income workers, not just Rowntree employees, and rents were to be kept low.

Fruit trees were planted in every garden, at Joseph Rowntree's insistence, and each dwelling had enough land to grow vegetables. The deeds of the village protected the many open green spaces around the project and all grass verges had trees planted in them.

The brickworks, which provided the raw materials for the houses, was on the outskirts of the village but closed in 1950. It is now a nature reserve.

HOME IMPROVEMENTS

By the middle of the decade, innovations which had seemed too expensive for the masses ten years before, were becoming increasingly popular. Electric lights, for example, were falling in price as more and more areas were connected to a public electricity supply, negating the need for a costly generator. In 1904, German architect Hermann Muthesius published *The English House,* in which he reported that electric light was 'becoming more and more general'.

In the same publication Muthesius praised the fitted bathrooms which were becoming increasingly familiar in middle-class homes. 'English fittings are celebrated everywhere,' he commented, adding that a well equipped bathroom should have a bath, a shower-bath, a hip-bath, a heated towel rail and a mirror – but no lavatory. Those who could afford indoor facilities were likely to have a separate WC, said Muthesius, commenting, 'a lavatory is practically never found in an English bathroom.'

HOUSEHOLD ROUTINE

As well as describing the interiors of the well-to-do home in *The English House*, Muthesius revealed the everyday routines that were rigidly enforced in British society. Employed as a cultural attaché from 1896 to 1903, Muthesius threw himself into the niceties of London and was fascinated by rituals such as calling cards being left at 4 pm and holding 'at homes' in the evening.

'The most striking characteristic that the foreigner notices about the English is that their patterns of life are immutable and fixed for all time,' he observed. Nonetheless, he admired their attitude to visitors. 'It is amiably taken for granted that no special arrangements will be made for the visitor . . . everything goes on as usual and the visitor is spared the embarrassing feeling – that ultimately obliges him to leave – that he is upsetting the routine of the house. True courtesy lies in the very absence of conspicuous marks of it.'

A REVOLUTION IN TEA

New York tea and coffee merchant Thomas Sullivan became the first man to sell tea bags. Initially made from hand-sewn muslin bags, the laborious stitching was soon replaced with a machine.

In the same year, iced tea was served by Englishman Richard Blechynden at the World Fair in St Louis and among the many delicacies reportedly introduced there were hamburgers, Dr Pepper and waffle-style ice-cream cones.

The Changing Role of Women

LEAD US NOT INTO TEMPTATION

In Rome, controversial Pope Pius X upset the ladies by criticising low-cut evening gowns. Issuing instructions to the diplomats assigned to the Holy

See, he stated that no woman who wished to be considered a good Catholic should wear the risqué fashion in the presence of a cardinal or any high church dignitary. In retaliation, some diplomat wives vowed not to attend functions.

THE STRUGGLE CONTINUES

Suffragette Dora Montefiore took direct action against the government when she refused to pay her taxes until women were given the vote. Having been instrumental in securing the women's vote in Australia, the famous campaigner returned to London and later joined Emmeline Pankhurst's Women's Social and Political Union.

Her monetary protest was thwarted when bailiffs seized her property and auctioned off enough to cover the bill, despite loud demonstration from suffragettes in the audience at the auction.

The following year, Dora was to protest in the same way, with similar results. But in 1906 the women of the movement gathered at her house when the bailiffs arrived and barred them from entry. The house was under siege for six weeks before the bailiffs broke down the doors and seized furniture, attracting much publicity for the cause.

Dora was later jailed for a separate demonstration after refusing to be bound over to keep the peace.

Elsewhere, the Equal Pay League was founded as part of the National Union of Teachers. Two years later, the organisation was renamed the National Federation of Women Teachers. In 1961, after equal pay was achieved, the union disbanded.

SMALL STEPS FORWARD

Electrical engineer Hertha Ayrton became the first woman to read her own paper, *The Origin and Growth of Ripple-mark,* at the world's oldest scientific academy, the Royal Society. Two years earlier, she had been nominated as the first female Fellow of the Royal Society but, on advice from the legal counsel, the institution did not allow her to be elected, and the honour was withdrawn.

In 1906, the Society awarded her the prestigious Hughes Medal for her experiments concerning the electric arc.

In Dublin, as a gesture to female students, Trinity College Dublin awarded BA and MA degrees to all the women who had passed exams at Oxford or Cambridge but who were barred from graduating. The practice continued for three years and the students earned the nickname 'steamboat ladies' because they usually stayed one night in the city before returning to England as soon as possible by steamboat.

Science

FIRST POLITICAL RECORDING

Kaiser Wilhelm of Germany made the first political recording, on March 3, on an Edison cylinder.

FATHER OF THE ATOMIC BOMB

US physicist J. Robert Oppenheimer – the 'father of the atomic bomb' – was born on April 22. During World War II, he was director of the Manhattan Project, which developed the first nuclear weapons.

Oppenheimer was shocked by the weapon's killing power after it was used to destroy the Japanese cities of Hiroshima and Nagasaki.

NEW VALVE HERALDS RADIO BREAKTHROUGH

Electrical engineer and physicist, John Fleming, of London University, invented a valve for electricity, allowing it to flow in one direction but not another. He called it the oscillation valve. It was a major breakthrough in radio technology, later replacing the unreliable crystal and cat's whisker combination.

Fleming, who was from Lancaster, lectured at several universities and was consultant to the Marconi Wireless Telegraph Company and the Edison Telephone Company. His diode was used in radio receivers and radars for many decades afterwards

A CLOSE SHAVE

King C Gillette patented the double-edged razor blade and sales of his safety razor soared.

Gillette's disposable razor was a unique invention that revolutionised the shaving industry. Born in Wisconsin, King became a travelling salesman. One morning, while shaving prior to going to work, he became irritated that his 'cut-throat razor' was blunt and so worn out that he couldn't sharpen it.

Gillette had a flash of inspiration. Instead of stropping and honing a razor, a disposable one would make life easier. It could also be made safer to use.

Together with his inventor partner William Emery Nickerson, they worked on the design but it took them several years to find someone who could provide a machine to sharpen thin sheets of metal for the blades.

They eventually perfected a safety razor blade, which could fit into a specially designed holder with a handle and an adjustable head.

Production began in 1903; Gillette introduced the double-edged blade a year later and changed the company name from the American Safety Razor Company to the Gillette Safety Razor Company.

Gillette was to become something of a celebrity after he put his face and signature on every package of razor blades.

PAVLOV'S DOG

Russian physiologist Ivan Pavlov received the Nobel Prize on December 10 for his research into how digestion works.

He discovered that nerve messages transmitted via the brain play an important part in the digestion process. When he severed a dog's gullet, the food it chewed never reached its stomach but digestive juices still flowed. He also found that if a bell is regularly rung when a dog is fed, the animal eventually salivates at the sound alone.

FIRST 'RADAR' DETECTED

German engineer Christian Hülsmeyer found a way of discovering 'the presence of distant metallic objects via radio waves', which led to the invention of radar.

After a friend died in a ship collision, Hülsmeyer was inspired to create a device that could detect ships and help prevent such disasters. In 1904, when he received a patent for the device, he successfully demonstrated that it could detect the presence of a ship in dense fog – although not how far away it was.

However, the German navy was unimpressed, and none of the European shipping lines he approached wanted to use his invention. It would be several years before others perfected radar and appreciated its capability.

Chapter Six

1905

Politics

WAR BETWEEN RUSSIA AND JAPAN IS ENDED

PRESIDENT ROOSEVELT offered to mediate in the war between Russia and Japan and the two countries agreed to hold peace talks in Washington. The war officially ended on September 5, with the signing of a peace treaty at Portsmouth, New Hampshire.

Under the terms of the agreement, known as the Treaty of Portsmouth, Russia agreed to evacuate troops from Manchuria and to recognise the exclusive rights of Japan in Korea.

LORD CURZON RESIGNS

Lord Curzon resigned as Viceroy of India on August 20, after clashing with the British military Commander-in-Chief in India, Lord Kitchener.

Curzon's resignation came after the Cabinet refused to appoint Major-General Barrow as Military Supply member of his council. It was the latest in a string of disagreements between Lord Curzon and the government and his resignation was readily accepted. He returned to England and was replaced by the Earl of Minto.

Lord Curzon resigned after clashes with Kitchener (pictured) and lack of support from the Cabinet.

TALK OF REVOLUTION IN RUSSIA

In the wake of civil unrest, demonstrations, a general strike and talk of revolution, Tsar Nicholas II took a half-hearted step towards a constitutional monarchy.

A new representative assembly was set up, called the Duma, the Russian word for 'deliberation'. The Tsar's 'October manifesto' also promised Russians civil rights such as freedom of conscience, speech, assembly and association.

But the reforms were greeted coolly by the people. The Duma was only a consultative body and many Russians felt that this did not go far enough. Leon Trotsky, the leader of the St Petersburg Soviet of Workers' Deputies, and other revolutionaries denounced the plan. Trotsky urged other workers' councils to begin arming themselves in preparation for a revolution.

PM RESIGNS

The Prime Minister, Arthur Balfour, was forced to resign on December 5, following his disastrous tariff reform which split the party.

With no government in place, King Edward VII invited Sir Henry Campbell-Bannerman, the Liberal leader, to form a new government.

Edward VII invited the Liberal leader, Sir Henry Campbell-Bannerman to form a government after Balfour's resignation.

Royalty

Grand Duke Sergei Alexandrovich, uncle of Tsar Nicholas II and one of his most influential advisors, was killed by an assassin in February.

As his carriage was coming out of the gates of the Kremlin, a bomb was thrown in by a socialist revolutionary terrorist, Ivan Kalyayev, blowing him to pieces.

The death was dramatically to change the life of the Duke's widow, Elizabeth, the Grand Duchess of Russia. She turned to prayer and fasting and walked away from her life of luxury. Full of compassion, she visited her husband's killer in prison and suggested he repent and find salvation.

She later took the vows of a nun and established a convent in Moscow and a hospital where she and her fellow nuns served. They also gave shelter to orphans and homeless people.

After the 1917 Revolution, when the Bolsheviks seized power, the Orthodox Church was seen as part of the old regime and so was persecuted.

Hundreds of priests and nuns were imprisoned, taken away to distant labour camps, and killed. Elizabeth was amongst them.

In 1984 she was recognised as a saint by the Russian Orthodox Church Abroad, and then by the Moscow Patriarchate in 1992.

Historical Events

RUSSIANS BLOODIED AND BATTERED AT HOME AND ABROAD

A succession of military defeats to Japan in the war over imperial rights in Korea and Manchuria, left the Russian people crushed and humiliated.

At home, strikers marched through St Petersburg to petition the Tsar for better conditions. Their way was blocked by a line of infantry which, without warning, opened fire, shooting down more than 500 men, women and children. The snow-covered ground was soaked in blood and the shocking incident became known as 'Bloody Sunday'.

In May, Admiral Togo of Japan was hailed a hero for his brilliant naval victory over the Russian Fleet in the Baltic. The Russian ships had sailed halfway round the world to protect their imperial interests but Togo's fleet was waiting for them as they emerged from the fog in the Strait of Tsushima.

Out of a total of 38 Russian ships, all but three were sunk, disabled or captured. An estimated 4,800 Russians perished in the encounter, compared with Japanese losses of three torpedo boats and 117 sailors.

NORTH WEST PASSAGE

Norwegian explorer Roald Amundsen became the first person successfully to sail through the Northwest Passage between the Atlantic and Pacific Oceans.

It had been something that explorers had been attempting to do since the days of Columbus and had claimed the lives of many sailors.

Amundsen's two-and-a-half-year voyage along America's frozen Arctic coast, from the Atlantic to Pacific, in search of the Passage, ended with his arrival at Fort Egbert, Alaska, on December 6.

Social Change

RELIEF FOR THE UNEMPLOYED

In June, 500 unemployed workers marched from Leicester to London to highlight their frustration at not being able to find work. Although the King refused to see them, the weary men were greeted in Trafalgar Square by a huge crowd who showered them with coins. The march hastened the passing of an act which was to recognise their plight.

The Unemployed Workmen's Act, passed by the Conservative Government, set up a 'distress committee' which had the power to award grants to businesses which wanted to hire more workers. This led to a significant decrease in unemployment.

SHORTER HOURS FOR MINER MINORS

A bill to give miners under 18 a maximum eight-hour day received its second reading in the House of Commons. Forty-three million tons of coal were produced in this year but it was also a year of tragedy for the industry. In March, 32 miners were killed in South Wales and in July, 124 more died in a Glamorgan pit disaster.

Elsewhere, trade unions called for an eight-hour day for all workers, as well as backing universal suffrage and old age pensions.

DR BARNADO'S LEGACY

On September 19, Irish doctor and philanthropist Thomas Barnado died. His experiences as a doctor in the East End of London had driven him to set up an organisation to provide shelter and education for deprived children: at the time of his death, 112 institutions had been established. Many of the needy children were sent abroad for a 'better life' with over 17,000 emigrating to Canada. Dr Barnado's homes claimed that no child in need was ever turned away.

AMBULANCES FOR ACCIDENT VICTIMS

In December, London County Council set up the first motorised ambulance service for victims of traffic accidents. Previously, victims had relied on stretchers and police vehicles, with ambulances used only for the isolation of those suffering from infectious diseases. The LCC plan was to provide two-wheeled carts and two motor ambulances which could be summoned by telephone.

OTHER EVENTS

A huge crowd lined the streets of Dover in August to see 'God's General' ,William Booth, the leader of the Salvation Army, embark on the first leg of his motor tour. The crusade, to last 40 days and 40 nights, aimed to encourage troops and renew the country's enthusiasm for religion.

In February an outbreak of typhus hit the East End and in September, Government figures showed a sharp rise in 'rural lunacy' which they blamed on the tedium of country life!

General Booth, the leader of the Salvation Army, echoed Christ's 40 days in the wilderness with his 40-day motor car tour, intended to encourage troops and revive the nation's interest in religion.

Fashion

In May and June, France was buzzing with news that the young King of Spain, Alphonso XIII, was attending the annual Paris fashion season. The 19-year-old monarch was the most eligible bachelor in Europe and was renowned for having an eye for the ladies.

On June 16, the *Washington Post* reported:

> *The merry-go-round of the Paris season has been an even madder whirl than usual this year, and reports of the toilettes worn at the various June fashion events in and near Paris are enthusiastic and exclamatory. Among other things, Paris has been entertaining a King – a young King, a King who smiled with boyish appreciation at*

Fashion continued to be as important as ever to Edwardian women with cinched in waists and long skirts but new press fasteners enabled more two-piece outfits and blouses to be worn, such as this design by Mr Collins.

pretty women and their chiffons, and the pretty women brought out their most ravishing chiffons to do him honor.

The handsome young royal clearly enjoyed the company of French women – the same year saw the birth of his first illegitimate child, to aristocrat Mélanie de Gaufridy de Dortan – but his heart would soon belong to an English princess.

After Paris he left for a state visit to the UK, where he met Queen Victoria's granddaughter, Princess Victoria Eugenie of Battenburg, also known as Ena. The young couple were married the following year and went on to have seven children.

A HOUSEHOLD NAME IS BORN

On January 21, Christian Dior was born in the seaside town of Gran-ville, France. The second of five children of Alexandre Dior, a wealthy fertiliser manufacturer, Christian was destined to become one of the most influential fashion designers of the forties and fifties.

Also in 1905, a new fashion saw press-fasteners introduced to hold the bodice or blouse to the skirt, paving the way for more two-piece outfits.

Entertainment

THEATRE

The Scarlet Pimpernel opened at the New Theatre, London, on January 5 and begun a popular run of 122 performances. The elusive English aristocrat who mocked the revolutionaries spawned the catchphrase 'they seek him here, they seek him there', and the novel, published soon after the play opened was a worldwide hit. The character's creator, Baroness Orczy, was to write many sequels in the following years.

W.B. Yeats' play *On Baile's Strand* opened at St George's Hall, London, in November.

In October, theatre lovers mourned the loss of Sir Henry Irving, the greatest actor of his time. Born in Somerset, he made his stage debut in 1865 and six years later became a household name with his portrayal of a tortured murderer in *The Bells*, at London's Lyceum theatre. His long running partnership with Ellen Terry proved a huge success both in the UK and the US and he was the first actor to receive a knighthood. He died aged 67, at the height of his popularity, and was buried in Westminster Abbey.

THE SUN RISES IN PARIS

Producer and actor Fred Terry as the 'damned elusive Pimpernel' who defied the revolutionaries to rescue members of the French aristocracy during the French Revolution in Baroness Orczy's famous creation which opened in London in January after a rewrite when it's original 1903 production failed to storm the West End.

On May 13, Dutch beauty Gertrud Margaretha Zelle, otherwise known as Mata Hari, made her stage debut at the Musée Guimet in Paris. Having left a husband and child behind in the Netherlands, she adopted her stage name from the Indonesian word meaning 'Sun', literally translated as 'eye of the day.'

Mata Hari's exotic dance act was an overnight sensation and she quickly became one of the most celebrated dancers – and courtesans – in Paris. Her legendary powers of seduction brought her wealth, status and a string of lovers which included millionaires, politicians and even the German

Crown Prince. Crucially, she also had affairs with some high-ranking military officers and, during the First World War, this and her free movement across Europe as a Dutch citizen, aroused the suspicion of the French intelligence.

In 1917 a German radio operator transmitted messages about a spy, alias H-21, in a code which had already been cracked by the French. The security services identified the spy as Mata Hari and in October, at the age of 41, she was executed by firing squad.

SUPERMAN SHAW

George Bernard Shaw dominated the London stage as well as the headlines. In March, his satire on Anglo- Irish relations, *John Bull's Other Island*, was a great success at the Court Theatre, where the King reportedly laughed so heartily he broke his chair.

On May 23, Shaw's *Man and Superman* opened to rave reviews and in November *Major Barbara* delivered a social message about the plight of the poor through the eyes of a Salvation Army officer heroine.

But it was not all good news for the Irish playwright. On November 1, the New York production of *Mrs Warren's Profession* was closed down by police and the actors arrested. The play, which centres on a prostitute's relationship with her prudish daughter, had twice been refused a licence by the Lord Chamberlain in the UK on the grounds of decency and had only been performed in private clubs. The magistrate adjourned the case while he read the offending material.

A frustrated Shaw commented: 'I have no wrath but a very great pity for all those foolish people. Prostitution is a permissible subject on the stage only when it is made agreeable. Why didn't they arrest the whole audience?'

FILM

Pathé Frères, the film production company run by Charles, Émile, Théophile and Jacques Pathé, became the first to add colour to a black and white film by machine.

MUSIC

The one-act opera *Salome* was performed for the first time, on December 9, at the Hofoper in Dresden. Written by Richard Strauss, it is based on the play by Oscar Wilde and is famous for the mysterious and seductive *Dance of the Seven Veils*.

Still from the film *Rescued by Rover*, a film by Ceil Hepworth which saw the first ever British film star – the collie, Blair who played Rover.

In London's Covent Garden, Puccini's opera *Madame Butterfly* had its first UK performance. In Vienna *The Merry Widow*, by Franz Lehàr, opened at the Theater an der Wien and was to become one of the most popular operettas of its time.

Popular songs of 1905 included *Wait 'Til the Sun Shines, Nellie* by Andrew B. Sterling and Harry Von Tilzer; *Waiting At The Church* by Fred W. Leigh and Henry E. Pether, and *How'd you Like to Spoon with Me* – Jerome Kern's first hit.

BIRTHS

January 26 – Maria Von Trapp, singer and inspiration for *The Sound of Music*.
March 18 – Robert Donat, English actor.
March 23 – Joan Crawford, US actress.
May 16 – Henry Fonda, US actor.
July 9 – Clara Bow, US actress and original 'It Girl'.

August 2 – Myrna Loy, US actress.
September 18 – Greta Garbo, Swedish actress.
November 15 – Annunzio Mantovani, Italian composer.
November 19 – Tommy Dorsey, jazz musician and brother of Jimmy.
November 21 – Ted Ray, comedian and violinist.

DEATHS

May 31 – Franz Strauss, musician and composer, father of Richard Strauss.
October 13 – Sir Henry Irving, actor.

Literature

THE GREAT DETECTIVE RETURNS

Twelve years after he supposedly fell to his death at the Reichenbach Falls, along with his arch enemy Moriarty, Sherlock Holmes was resurrected in book form. *The Return of Sherlock Holmes,* by Sir Arthur Conan Doyle, was a collection of 13 stories published in *The Strand* magazine the year before, after intense pressure from his fans. In the first, *The Adventure of the Empty House,* Sherlock has been 'dead' for three years but appears in Dr Watson's study and explains that he survived the fall but has had to stay away to escape Moriarty's henchmen.

THE DEATH OF A FUTURIST

On March 24, at the age of 79, novelist Jules Verne died at his home in the French town of Amiens. The son of an attorney, born in Nantes, Verne was a visionary whose futuristic novels earned him the title of the 'Father of Science Fiction' (also often applied to his contemporary H.G.Wells). He envisaged air, space and underwater travel long before aeroplanes, submarines and spacecraft were invented. In *Paris in the Twentieth Century,* a novel written in 1863 which went unpublished until 1989, Verne's vision of the city included skyscrapers, gas-powered cars, calculators and high speed trains.

The most famous of Jules Verne's novels remain *Journey to the Centre of the Earth, Twenty Thousand Leagues Under the Sea* and *Around the World in Eighty Days.*

OTHER MAJOR WORKS

Five years after his death, Oscar Wilde's 50,000-word letter to former lover Lord Alfred Douglas was published as *De Profundis*. Wilde wrote the heartfelt missive during his time in prison but was not permitted to send it. On his release, he gave it to his friend Robert Ross and asked that a copy be sent to Douglas. While Douglas claimed never to have received it, Ross published an edited version of the manuscript in 1905, and included it in a collected works volume in 1908. Douglas then donated it to the British Museum on the understanding it would not be made public until 1960. The complete version was published in 1962.

Also published this year were Frances Hodgson Burnett's *A Little Princess*, Baroness Orczy's *The Scarlet Pimpernel* and H.G. Wells, *Kipps*, later to become the inspiration for the musical *Half a Sixpence*.

BIRTHS

May 16 – H.E. Bates, British novelist.
October 15 – C. P. Snow, British novelist.
December 21 – Anthony Powell, British novelist.

DEATHS

February 15 – General Lew Wallace, author of *Ben-Hur: A Tale of the Christ.*
March 25 – Jules Verne.

Architecture

EXPRESS YOURSELF

Europe saw the emergence of 'Expressionist architecture' with German, Dutch, Austrian, Czech and Danish schools leading the way. The designs leaned towards a modern look, using new mass-produced materials such as steel and glass. The shapes were sometimes based on a distortion of natural lines, while others were inspired by the technological advances of the age. The idea was that the form of the building could evoke or express strong feelings.

Although the term was initially used around 1910, retrospective studies have identified works as early as 1905 as 'Expressionist'.

ALDWYCH AND KINGSWAY

London County Council's first urban improvement scheme opened, hailing a new era for planning in the capital.

The increase in traffic in the city had led to calls for a new road between Holborn and Fleet Street: the Council, established in 1889, took up the scheme. The slums which blighted the Strand were cleared away and a crescent was designed around the historic church of St Clement Danes.

Kingsway, named in honour of Edward VII, was the widest road in London, at 30 metres (100 feet) and boasted a tunnel underneath for the electric tram. Plots of land either side of the road were leased to builders for the construction of business properties with the intention of creating a new commercial district.

BERLINER DOM

After ten years of work, the Berliner Dom, or Berlin Cathedral, was completed. Designed by Julius Raschdorff in the baroque style, it was built on orders of the German Emperor Wilhelm II as a protestant answer to St Peter's Basilica in Rome. The new cathedral, 114 metres long, 73 metres wide and 116 metres tall, stands on an island in the river Spree.

Art

ART GOES WILD

Fauvism, a short-lived but influential art movement, was born in France. The name, derived from the French word 'fauve', meaning 'wild beast', was coined by the critic Louise Vauxelles and was intended as an insult. However, the wildly experimental group of artists to whom he was referring cheerfully adopted it as their own.

The style of the Fauvists was essentially expressionist, with unconventional colours and distorted forms. Henri Matisse, Maurice Vlamnick and Andre Derain are the best-known of the group, with Matisse causing a huge stir in critical circles with his painting, *Green Strip*. This fairly traditional portrait of his wife was rendered dramatically unorthodox when he painted her nose green.

The critically condemned movement was to last only four years but it proved hugely successful with the public and went on to influence many styles in Modern Art, including Cubism.

PICASSO IN THE PINK

Picasso's three-year 'blue period' came to an end as he entered his 'rose period', characterised by lighter shades and more cheerful subject matter, such as harlequins and circus acts. Now living in Paris full-time, he had formed a relationship with Fernande Olivier, his first great love, and his new happiness was reflected in his optimistic style.

Paintings from this year include *Portrait of Madame Canals* and *Woman with a Fan*. Another 1905 work, *Garçon a la Pipe* (Or Boy with a Pipe), was sold in 2004 at Sotheby's in New York for $104 million (£58 million), making it the world's most expensive painting at the time.

THE NATIONAL ARTS COLLECTION

Two years after it was founded, the National Arts Collection Fund which collected and preserved art works for public viewing in the UK, made its first significant purchase. Whistler's *Nocturne in Blue and Gold* was presented to the National Gallery of British Art, now known as the Tate Gallery.

The British warship, HMS King Edward VII was completed in February, although she was actually launched in 1903, and became the flag ship to the Channel Fleet in 1907. She sank on 6th January, 1916, 12 hours after being mined off Cape Wrath.

DEATHS

May 23 – Paul Dubois, French painter and sculptor.
Date unknown – Jean-Baptiste Guillaume, French sculptor.

Travel and Transport

DRIVE ON CARS

The year saw a steep interest in cars. No longer were they considered to be the playthings of hobbyists and enthusiasts; now they were attracting the attention of those who saw them as convenient and effective forms of transport.

This year's Motor Show, at Olympia in London, was the biggest yet, attracting huge crowds. The Prince and Princess of Wales had a preview and the PM, Arthur Balfour, and the Foreign Secretary, Lord Lansdowne, attended on the opening day.

AA FOUNDED

Despite the interest in cars, there remained some prejudice against them in Britain. Many car owners felt that the police were overly keen to catch them speeding.

On June 29, a group of around 50 motoring enthusiasts met at the Trocadero restaurant in London to form the Automobile Association. All agreed to pay an annual subscription of two guineas to support the association. Its main task was to help motorists avoid the increasingly widespread speed-traps, in which policemen often used conventional stopwatches to estimate car speeds.

Anyone driving above the 20 mph legal speed limit was arrested, although motorists claimed the tests were wildly inaccurate.

WINDSHIELD WIPERS PATENTED

While travelling in a tram in New York, Mary Anderson, originally from Alabama, had noticed that the driver had to stop periodically and wipe the windows so that he could see ahead. She later noticed that car drivers had the same problem.

Mary went home, started experimenting and eventually came up with the idea of rubber blades attached to a spring-loaded arm. A lever inside the car caused the blades to wipe across the windscreen and the spring returned them to the original position. The idea won her a patent in 1905.

Toys

The popularity of teddy bears spread around the world and led to many other soft toy animals being produced, including dogs, cats, elephants, lions and tigers.

A cinnamon coloured mohair Steiff teddy 'girl' bear made in 1905 was auctioned in London in 1994. It was sold for a record price for an antique bear of £110,000. The new owner was Yoshiro Sekiguchi, the co-founder of the Teddy Bear Museum in Japan.

Sport

THE COMMON TOUCH

Footballer Alf Common became the most expensive player to date when he was transferred for a fee of £1,000.

Common, from Tyne and Wear, joined Sunderland in 1900 and then Sheffield United. When the England international wanted to return home, he re-joined Sunderland in the summer of 1904.

In February 1905, little more than six months after this move, he was transferred to Middlesbrough for a record breaking four-figure sum. He proved his worth in his first game for Middlesbrough on February 25, away to his former club Sheffield United. Middlesbrough won 1–0, with Common scoring from a penalty after 50 minutes. It was their first away win for nearly two years.

BOXING LEGEND LOSES CROWN

Bob Fitzsimmons lost his light-heavyweight crown on December 20 to Jack O'Brien from Philadelphia, one of the fastest fighters of his day. The fight was stopped in the thirteenth round in San Francisco.

Born in Cornwall, Fitzsimmons moved to New Zealand with his parents when he was still a child. His name became legendary after a remarkable career that saw him capture world titles in three divisions – middleweight, light-heavyweight and heavyweight.

RECORD US OPEN WIN FOR ANDERSON

Willie Anderson won the US Open for a record fourth time. Anderson was born in North Berwick, Scotland and emigrated to the US when he was 16. His record achievement was equalled 25 years later by Bobby Jones, then Ben Hogan and Jack Nicklaus.

SHOCK WIN AT WIMBLEDON

British dominance in the ladies' singles tennis championships at Wimbledon was interrupted by the victory of US player May Sutton, who defeated the reigning champion, Dorothea Douglass, 6–3, 6–4.

The 19-year-old was born in Plymouth but moved with her parents to a ranch near Pasadena, California, when she was six. She played tennis with her three sisters on a court built by their father, and the girls dominated the California tennis circuit. In 1904 she won the singles title at the US Championships.

NEW FOOTBALL TEAMS KICK-OFF

The year saw the founding of both Chelsea and Charlton Athletic football clubs. Chelsea's new ground at Stamford Bridge attracted a lot of players from local teams. Originally an athletics stadium, it was able to accommodate vast attendances. The team started its life in Division Two but only two years later Chelsea were promoted to Division One, as Division Two runners-up behind Nottingham Forest.

Charlton Athletic FC was formed by a boys' club; during their formative years playing at the valley there was a lack of facilities at the ground and they often used a local fishmongers shop to get changed for their games! This is said to be the reason why the team acquired their nickname 'The Addicks' – a corruption of Haddock.

The Home

A SERVANTS' LOT

In the 1905 book *A Little Princess*, Frances Hodgson Burnett describes a servant's attic bedroom, undoubtedly similar to those found in almost any upper-class home:

Yes, this was another world. The room had a slanting roof and was whitewashed. The whitewash was dingy and had fallen off in places. There was a rusty grate, an old iron bedstead, and a hard bed covered with a faded coverlet. Some pieces of furniture too much worn to be used downstairs had been sent up. Under the skylight in the roof, which showed nothing but an oblong piece of dull gray sky, there stood an old battered red footstool.

While some families got by with one or two maids, the wealthier houses required an army of domestic servants to run smoothly and that meant a hefty wage bill. Below is a table of servants' wages in 1905 (according to Channel Four's *Edwardian House*) and how much that equates to in 2007.

Butler	£60	£3483
Housekeeper	£45	£2612
Chef	£80	£4644
Ladies maid	£32	£1858
Kitchen maid	£24	£1393
First footman	£26	£1509
Second footman	£24	£1393
First housemaid	£28	£1625
Second housemaid	£22	£1277
Scullery maid	£12	£697
Coachman	£18	£1045
Hallboy	£16	£929

However, a housemaid or servant was becoming an unattainable luxury to many of the middle classes. As Methesius reported in *The English Terraced House,* many bemoaned the fact that, with new career opportunities in shops and offices, '£20 maids' were hard to come by.

In terms of house design, this, and the preference for fewer children than in the Victorian era, led to smaller, more affordable homes being built and a cosier style of interior decoration.

COUNTRY LIVING

The report on *Agricultural Labourers' Wages* showed that the average weekly wage for a farmhand was 18/3d, around £361 in today's terms. Of that 1/- to 2/6d went to cottage rental and the majority of the rest, 13/6½d went towards food.

The Changing Role of Women

WOMEN ARE TALKED OUT

The 'Women's Political and Social Union' (WSPU) persuaded sympathetic MP John Bamford Slack to introduce a women's suffrage bill, drafted by its members.

Under the rules of Westminster, if MPs are talking when the House is set to adjourn, any legislation in debate is lost. On May 12, the bill was met with laughter, high tempers and some interruption from the public gallery before being 'talked out'.

One MP commented that 'men and women differ in mental equipment with, women having little sense of proportion'.

WSPU UP THE STAKES

As a result of the disappointing reception of the women's suffrage bill, the WSPU decided to adopt more aggressive tactics to put their point across. They pledged to attack whichever party was in government and refuse to support any social reform bills which did not include a move towards women's votes.

Direct action was also called for. Christabel Pankhurst and Annie Kenney hit the headlines when they interrupted a meeting in Manchester to ask Liberal MPs Winston Churchill and Sir Edward Grey if they agreed women should be allowed to vote. When they received no reply, they unfurled a 'Votes for Women' banner, shouted at the two men and were promptly arrested.

Both women chose to go to prison rather than pay a fine for causing an obstruction and assaulting a police officer.

Emmeline Pankhurst, Christabel's mother, later wrote in her auto-biography, 'This was the beginning of a campaign the like of which was never known in England, or for that matter in any other country . . . we interrupted a great many meetings . . . and we were violently thrown out and insulted. Often we were painfully bruised and hurt.'

PEACE AND JUSTICE

In December, the annual Nobel Peace Prize was awarded to Baroness Bertha von Suttner, the first woman to receive the honour. The Austrian novelist and passionate pacifist had worked as Alfred Nobel's secretary for a week in 1876, before running off to marry Arthur von Suttner, but kept a regular correspondence with Nobel until his death 20 years later. It is thought that it was her suggestion that he include a peace prize in his plans for the annual awards.

In 1889, Bertha published the anti-war novel *Die Waffen Neider! (Lay Down Your Arms)* and two years later she founded the Austrian Peace Society, of which she was a long-term president. Soon afterwards she started a peace journal, named after her novel, which she was to edit for seven years. Now regarded as a national hero, Baroness Suttner's image appears on the two Euro coin in Austria.

Science

EINSTEIN'S WONDERFUL YEAR

German physicist Albert Einstein made 1905 a huge year in physics with the publication of four brilliant papers – the most startling being his 'special theory of relativity', which argued that time and space are not constant. This undermined the classical laws of physics and introduced a modern way of looking at the universe. It also introduced the idea that everything is relative.

Einstein deduced from his equations of special relativity what later became the most famous mathematical equation in science: $E = mc2$, suggesting that tiny amounts of mass could be converted into huge amounts of energy.

His other papers this year showed how light interacts with matter as 'packets' (quanta) of energy. He also explained the random movement of very small objects as direct evidence of molecular action, thus supporting the atomic theory.

These historic documents were to become known as the Annus Mirabilis Papers.

BAKELITE INVENTED

Belgium chemist Leo Baekeland invented the first synthetic material – the forerunner of plastic.

A keen photographer, he had already invented the first commercially successful photographic paper, the process for which he sold to George Eastman in 1898 for a whopping $1 million.

In 1905, he found that when he combined formaldehyde and phenol, he produced a material that bound all types of powders together. He called it Bakelite, after himself.

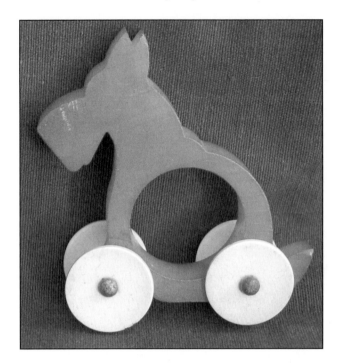

Bakelite was invented by the Belgian chemist Leo Baekeland. It came into its own in the Art Deco period when this collectable box was created and there were more colours available than the original black.

This was a material that, once it set hard, would not soften under heat. It was water and solvent resistant, could be used as an electrical insulator and could be moulded into all sorts of shapes and sizes. It had so much potential that it was called 'the material of a thousand uses'.

INTELLIGENCE TEST

French psychologist Alfred Binet invented an intelligence test that was the basis of today's IQ test.

His principal goal was to identify students who needed special help in coping with the school curriculum. Along with his collaborator Théodore Simon, they developed a test primarily for children aged three to 15 that would compare their intellectual capabilities with other children of the same ages.

In 1905, Prole claimed that he and Frank McCarthy broadcast voices between stations in San Francisco, an early radio broadcast. (Image courtesy of the Estate of Stanley Shoop).

SF 189054
DEFENITELY FIXES RADIO'S "BIRTHDAY"
RADIO WAS OFFICIALLY "BORN" ON DECEMBER 21, 1912 DECLARES
WILLIAM A PROLE (ABOVE) AFTER MONTHS OF RESEARCH IN
THE LIBRARY OF THE UNIVERSITY OF CALIFORNIA. PROLE
DECLARES THAT HE ASSISTED THE LATE FRANCIS MCCARTHY
IN EXPERIMENTAL WORK IN SAN FRANCISCO AND THAT THEY
BROADCAST VOICES BETWEEN STATIONS A MILE APART IN 1905.
ACCORDING TO PROLE, THE FIRST OFFICIAL BROADCAST WAS
FROM LOS ANGELES TO THE NAVAL WIRELESS STATION AT PT.
LOMA, CAL., A DISTANCE OF 135 MILES, ON DEC. 21, 1912.
CREDIT LINE(ACME)   5/31/32

Chapter Seven

1906

Politics

EMERGING WORLD POWER

ENCOURAGED by their impressive military and naval success against Russia in the conflict over Korea and Manchuria, Japan announced plans to almost double the size of its navy by 1908. Shortly after this proud and bold claim by the emerging global power, the British government declared that its Navy budget would be £1.5m, lower than 1905.

LANDSLIDE VICTORY FOR LIBERALS

On February 7, the Liberals were formally confirmed in power after a landslide General Election victory. They had 399 MPs in the new Parliament, with the Tories trailing with 156.

One of the main reasons why they won so decisively is that voters feared there would be dearer food if the Tories were re-elected, as they gave preferential tariffs to trade from the Empire.

A strong working-class, anti-Tory movement saw the Liberals form a pact with the newly affiliated Labour Party – formerly the Labour Representation Committee – led by James Keir Hardie.

COLLAPSE OF RUSSIA'S NEW PARLIAMENT

Russia's first elected Parliament, the Duma, soon clashed with Tsar Nicholas II when it called for amnesty for political prisoners.

It was estimated that 1,000 political prisoners a day were being sent to exile in Siberia. On November 2, workers' leader Leon Trotsky was amongst those exiled to Siberia for life.

After further clashes, the Duma was dissolved by new Prime Minister Peter Stolypin, on July 21, and martial law declared.

BIRTHS

April 9 – British Labour Party leader Hugh Gaitskell.
December 19 – Soviet leader Leonid Brezhnev.

Royalty

ROYAL WEDDING ALMOST ENDS IN TRAGEDY

King Alphonso of Spain married Scottish-born Princess Victoria Eugenie of Battenberg – a grandaughter of Queen Victoria and niece of King Edward VII – on May 13.

The glittering ceremony at the Royal Monastery of San Geronimo in Madrid almost ended in tragedy as the King and his new bride, now called Queen Victoria, made their way back to the Royal Palace in an open carriage.

From his vantage point on a balcony overlooking the road the anarchist Mateu Morrall threw a bomb which was concealed inside a bouquet. The royal couple escaped injury as the bomb rolled
it killed 18 people and injured 30 others.

DEATHS

January 29 – King Christian IX of Denmark.

ATTEMPT
TO ASSASSINATE
THE
KING AND QUEEN
OF SPAIN.

INHUMAN OUTRAGE
AFTER THE WEDDING.

BOMB THROWN IN
A BOUQUET.

ROYAL COUPLE
UNINJURED.

EIGHT KILLED AND MANY
WOUNDED.

STATE COACH WRECKED.

COURAGE OF THE BRIDAL
PAIR.

ASSASSIN'S ESCAPE.

Playboy King Alfonso XII of Spain's wedding day to Edward VII's niece, Princess Victoria of Battenburg, was marred by an assassination attempt as recorded in this article in *The Daily Mail*.

Historical Events

ZULU UPRISING

A Zulu uprising against British rule met with a swift and brutal response when troops killed 60 of the rebels in March. The following month, the government sent a further 7,000 troops to South Africa, where they killed over 1,000 Zulus in fierce clashes.

MOUNT VESUVIUS ERUPTS

The intermittent eruptions from the Italian volcano Mount Vesuvius caused some concern among people living under its shadow.

The air of foreboding was shattered by a huge eruption on April 7. More than 100 people died and many more were injured from the molten lava and tremors which caused buildings to collapse.

SAN FRANCISCO DESTROYED BY EARTHQUAKE

Another devastating natural disaster occurred on April 18 when a major earthquake in San Francisco destroyed much of the city, killing at least 1,000 people.

Raging fires burnt buildings to the ground, claiming lives and causing horrific injuries. The water mains were also damaged, which meant that the city fire department had few resources with which to fight the fires.

Looters took advantage of the situation but they were ruthlessly dealt with. Soldiers, assisting police, were given orders to shoot to kill and it is estimated that as many as 500 people were shot dead in the city.

Thousands of citizens spent the night sleeping in parks or in tents on the outskirts of the city. Thousands more fled in ferries and trains as the fires continued to rage for four days.

Social Change

SCHOOL DINNERS

The new Liberal government was committed to reform to help the poorest members of society and especially to improve the health and welfare of children. One idea, the provision of meals at school, was not, however, met with universal approval: in April a headmaster told the Commons Select Committee that he thought the practice was unnecessary.

Bradford MP Fred Jowett, whose constituency had already started providing food illegally, made school meals the subject of his maiden speech. He convinced MPs that hungry children did not learn easily, and Parliament passed the Provision of School Meals Act. However, it was not compulsory and, 30 years later, only half of local authorities provided school dinners.

CADBURY FINDS LIFE IS NOT SO SWEET

Edward Cadbury and others carried out a study on wages of working class men and women in the Birmingham area. The authors found low pay and terrible working conditions in a number of industries, including the metal industry and the garment trade. They also found a vast inequality between the pay of men and women.

In the metal industry, for example, they found that, where women replaced men, they would get 'from one third to half the wages of a man'.

The same year, Mary MacArthur attempted to redress the balance by forming the National Federation of Women Workers, and the following year she founded the monthly newspaper *Women Worker*.

A LONG ROAD AHEAD

The new government still had a long way to go to improve the lives of the poor – and the population was growing. A study conducted by the University of London found that birth rates among the upper classes were dropping while poorer families had a higher birth rate.

David Lloyd George declared that sixty per cent of poverty in the UK was caused by drinking and gambling. 'Britain is the richest country under the sun yet it has 10 million workmen living in conditions of chronic destitution,' he told the Society for Social Service of North Wales Wesleyans' in September.

'Drink is the most urgent problem of the hour for our rulers to grapple with. Next year the government will wrestle with it in earnest and tackle the potent forces that profit from this degradation.'

Unemployment was a huge problem, especially outside of London. In February, a group of jobless men marched on London from the Midlands to highlight the problem.

Things were looking up, though, for those at the end of their working life, with Parliament approving the principle of an old age pension which would be paid for with taxes.

Workers taking a day out in London, whilst others marched from the Midlands in protest at high unemployment in an age before the Welfare State. In the background, new buildings are being erected and the Edwardian era was an unprecedented age for building, although there were still not enough jobs to go round.

Fashion

THE PRICE OF GLAMOUR

Ready to wear fashion was becoming increasingly popular amongst the middle classes as it was both stylish and affordable. But the glamorous outfits came at a high human cost, with most being produced in sweat-shops.

Workers in the 'sweated industries' often worked 13 to 14 hours a day in appalling conditions, many cramped workshops providing accommodation at night. Workers' pay was disproportionately small for the price of the garment. An intricate silk blouse, for example, might retail at around 18s but the worker would receive around 10d.

In an attempt to highlight the problem, journalist Richard Mudie Smith organised the *Daily News* 'Anti-Sweating Exhibition', supported by the paper's owners, the philanthropic Cadbury Brothers. Opened by Princess Henry of Battenburg on May 2, the exhibition ran for six weeks and attracted 30,000 visitors to London's Queen's Hall.

Detailed brochures were printed and 20,000 sold. The event put the issue of sweated labour firmly on the political agenda and led to the formation of the Anti-Sweating League, which aimed to establish a minimum wage in the UK.

SCHOOLGIRL FASHION

Responding to the need for more workers in the garment trade, Shoreditch Technical Institute founded a Girls' Trade School. Courses included dressmaking, embroidery and upholstery and the classes were two thirds trade orientated and one third general education.

Pupils were taken from the age of 12, for two years, and were trained to find work in the high-class couturiers of the West End. Day release courses also operated for those women already working in the industry.

In 1967, the Shoreditch Girls' Trade School merged with the Trade School for Girls, Barrett Street (founded 1915), to form the London School of Fashion.

GOOD HAIR DAY

German hairdresser Karl Nessler unveiled his permanent wave technique in October at a public demonstration in London. Despite the chemicals treatment consisting of cow's urine mixed with water, the 'perm' became an instant fashion hit. The 'spiral heat method' involved wrapping long hair around twelve brass rods connected to an electric heating device, applying the alkali chemicals and then heating at 212°F (100°C).

A system of weights was designed to keep the heated brass away from the head, although a few of the early customers suffered nasty burns to the scalp. In fact Nessler's long-suffering wife, Katharina, lost her hair twice in the experimental stages.

The electric permanent wave machine was patented in 1909 and women paid a fortune to have their hair done by the famous inventor himself.

Sadly, Nessler did not prove a lucky man. A resident in London since 1901 he was imprisoned in World War One because of his German nationality and all his assets were seized. After fleeing to America, he made a second fortune from his salons but was destined to lose it all in the crash of 1929. Shortly afterwards his house burned down.

Entertainment

FILM

Ten years since the Lumiere brothers showed their revolutionary film at the Empire in Leicester Square, the technology of the moving image had come on in leaps and bounds. The venues for audiences, however, had not.

Many were shown in theatres as part of a variety act, or were screened in empty shops with fold-up chairs. Fairgrounds were the only places you could find an area dedicated to 'bioscopes', with some booths accommodating up to a thousand.

In 1906, however, formal cinemas began to be built around the country and, while they were well constructed and comfortable, they increased the cost of admission considerably.

The world's first feature film, *The Story of the Kelly Gang*, was released in December. Made in Australia, at a cost of around $2,250 (£1,100), it was a biopic of legendary bushranger Ned Kelly and was an unprecedented 70 minutes long. Sadly, most of the film is now lost but, in November 2006, a 17 minute digital restoration was released by the National Film and Sound Archive.

Audiences were also treated to the first animated film, *Humorous Phases of Funny Faces* by American director Stuart J. Blackton. It featured an artist using a blackboard to draw faces, which then came to life, and an animated dog jumping through a hoop.

THEATRE

Controversial performer Isadora Duncan was banned from dancing in public in Berlin on the grounds that her act was 'obscene'. Isadora, who is credited with the introduction of modern dance, was the subject of a police order on January 4 which banned her from performing her act barefoot on the 'score of impropriety'.

In August, it was reported that Isadora had married her lover Gordon Craig, the son of actress Ellen Terry. In fact, the pair never wed but they did have a daughter, Deirdre, in September.

Although a celebrated artist in Europe, Isadora's life was beset with tragedy. Deirdre and her three-year-old brother Patrick drowned with their nanny in 1913 when the car they were in rolled into the Seine. Isadora was to die in 1927 when one of the many scarves she loved to wear caught in the wheel of a car driven by her lover, Benoît Falchetto.

Another controversial character, Henrik Ibsen, passed away in May. The Norwegian poet and playwright had revolutionised the theatre with his bleak and unromantic view of life and love. Ibsen had angered many with his brutal portrayal of society's ills in his 1880s plays *A Dolls House, Hedder Gabler* and *Ghosts*. The 1891 UK premiere of *Ghosts* was met with horror by one *Daily Telegraph* critic, who described it as: 'A disgusting representation. An open drain; a loathsome sore unbandaged; a dirty act done publicly' and 'Absolutely loathsome and fetid. . . . Crapulous stuff.'

However, Ibsen did have some high-profile supporters, most notably George Bernard Shaw, who saw him as a social reformer, and James Joyce, who published a glowing essay on his final work *When We Dead Awaken* in 1900.

Ibsen, who had not worked for six years due to a massive stroke, died on May 23 in his home city of Kristiana, now known as Oslo.

RADIO

Canadian Reginald Fessenden had been experimenting with radio, financed by the National Electric Signalling Company, since 1900. On Christmas Eve, he made a huge breakthrough when he transmitted the world's first radio programme from his work place at Brant Rock.

Amazed radio operators on ships in the Atlantic heard Fessenden play *O Holy Night* on the violin, make a speech, recite some poetry and read a passage from the Bible.

BIRTHS

February 10 – Lon Chaney Jnr, US actor.
March 6 – Lou Costello, US comedian of *Abbott and Costello* fame.
May 3 – Mary Astor, US actress and Oscar winner.
May 8 – Roberto Rossellini, Italian director.
June 3 – Josephine Baker, US-born dancer and jazz singer.
June 22 – Billy Wilder, US director.
July 3 – George Sanders, US actor.
August 5 – John Houston, US director and actor.
August 5 – Joan Hickson, UK actress.
October 6 – Janet Gaynor, US actress and first winner of Best Actress Oscar.
November 14 – Louise Brooks, US actress.
December 5 – Otto Preminger, Austrian director.
December 15 – Lew Grade, US producer.

DEATHS

May 23 – Henrik Ibsen, Norwegian poet and playwright.

Literature

A SAGA BEGINS

British novelist John Galsworthy published *A Man of Property,* the story of a wealthy businessman who strives to own everything he can but fails to possess his beautiful wife. The book introduced the Forsyte family, including the unhappy couple Soames and Irene, and was the first in the series which became known as *The Forsyte Saga.*

It was to be 15 years and a world war later before Galsworthy returned to the Forsyte family, with the short story *Indian Summer of Forsyte.* On reading it, his god-daughter remarked, 'Why not go on with them – give us more Forsytes?' This inspired him to plan a trilogy, he wrote to a friend: 'This idea, if I can ever bring it to fruition, will make *The Forsyte Saga* . . . the most sustained and considerable piece of fiction of our generation at least.'

Two further novels, *In Chancery* and *To Let,* were published in 1920 and 1921 and the saga spanned 34 years and three generations of the family. Further stories of the Forsytes appeared in *The White Monkey* (1924), *The Silver Spoon* (1926) and *Swan Song* (1928) and a collected version, *A Modern Comedy,* was published in 1929.

Although he came from a very wealthy background and wrote about upper class life, Galsworthy had a deep social conscience. His 1906 play *The Silver Box* revealed his anger at injustice in the relative treatments of the rich and poor in society.

In 1932, John Galsworthy won the Nobel Prize for Literature.

FANGS FOR THE MEMORY

White Fang, by American novelist and social reformer Jack London, was serialised in *The Outing Magazine* from May to October.

Three years after his most famous work *The Call of the Wild* described the journey of a pampered domestic dog as he learns to become a wild animal, the companion novel reversed the idea. *White Fang* was the tale of a wild wolf-like dog who is slowly domesticated.

London's stories, told through the dogs' eyes, explore the brutal world of the wild and the similarity of animal behaviour to that of 'civilised' humans.

A CHILDREN'S CLASSIC

The Railway Children, by E. Nesbit, was also published. A wealthy family are forced to move to a railway house after their father is imprisoned on an erroneous spying charge. Roberta, Peter and Phyllis befriend the station porter and a regular commuter, known as The Old Gentleman, who eventually helps to prove their father's innocence.

The story was adapted into a successful 1968 TV series and a 1970 film, both starring Jenny Agutter as Roberta.

BIRTHS

January 23 – Anya Seton, US author.
March 25 – A.J.P. Taylor, UK historian.
April 13 – Samuel Beckett, Irish playwright, winner of the 1969 Nobel
          Prize for Literature.
June 20 – Catherine Cookson, UK novelist.

Architecture

BRIDGE OVER TROUBLED WATERS

The bridge over the River Thames at Vauxhall, built in 1829, had to be demolished in 1898 to be replaced with a new design from Alexander Binnie. Opened in 1906 by the Prince of Wales, the bridge featured five arches with sculptures in each one. The upstream figures were provided by F.W. Pomeroy and those on the downstream by Alfred Drury.

Also in London, the Waldorf Hotel was built in the Aldwych and instantly became a meeting place for American businessmen. For this reason, the nearby development of Kingsway was soon to be populated with the British headquarters for US businesses.

WRIGHT'S RIGHT TO LIGHT

Frank Lloyd Wright's 'Robie House' became the most perfect example of the Prairie Style home that he had pioneered. The Chicago home was designed for engineer Frederick Robie, who wanted a maximum amount of light but no intrusion from neighbours.

Wright designed a huge cantilever that sheltered the living room from the sun, and a terrace or balcony on each level made up for a lack of garden. A central fireplace gave unity to the house. Wright designed every internal feature, from light fittings to rugs.

BIRTHS

July 8 – Philip Johnson, US architect.

Art

EXPOSITION FEVER

An article in the *New York Times* reported 'The year 1906 will go down in history as the year of expositions'. Seven World Fairs were planned in places as diverse as Santiago in Chile, Christchurch in New Zealand and Barcelona in Spain.

The highlight of the art calendar, however, was Milan's *Exposition Internationale.* As well as celebrating advances in technology, transport and industry, there was a huge display of artwork, sculpture and architecture.

Sadly, on August 2 a fire raged through the the Palace of Decorative Arts, damaging buildings and works, with a value between $2 million and $3 million (£1-£1.5 million) and completely destroying the section devoted to Italian decorative art and architecture. Next door the Pavilion of Fine Arts was saved, but many paintings were damaged by water and mud as firemen attempted to remove them.

CÉZANNE'S SACRIFICE

Getting caught in a storm while working on his latest masterpiece proved fatal to Paul Cézanne. The artist, regarded by many as the greatest of his time, was working in a field when a storm broke but continued his labours for two hours. He collapsed on his way home and was picked up by a passing driver and taken home, where he was revived by his housekeeper and sent to bed. The next day he was up and working again, but fainted and had to be put to bed. On October 22, he died of pneumonia at the age of 67.

Cezanne, who once stated his aim was to 'make Impressionism solid and enduring like the Old Masters', paved the way to a radically different style at the beginning of the Twentieth Century and laid the foundations of Cubism.

Hugely respected by his peers, he was dubbed 'My one and only master . . . the father of us all', by Picasso, who took Cezanne's own compositional structure and developed it into the Cubist style.

Cezanne painted landscapes, portraits and many still lifes, often reworking the same subjects, such as his famous still lifes with apples and oranges. In 1999, *Still life with curtain, pitcher and bowl of fruit* (1893–94) sold for a record $60.5 million (£37.8m) at Sotheby's in New York.

Milan's Exposition Internationale was marred by a fire which destroyed the displays of Italian decorative art and architecture but, despite this, it was a great success with 10 million visitors to the 100 hectare site. 25 countries participated in the seven-month fair with its theme of transport (Image courtesy of the Estate of Stanley Shoop).

RODIN'S MUSE

Welsh artist Gwen John began to model for Auguste Rodin, with whom she was having a passionate affair. Despite an age gap of 36 years, Gwen had fallen madly in love with the celebrated sculptor.

When she was not with her lover, she would sit in the café opposite his studio and even camp in the shrubbery at night. Rodin encouraged her in her work and helped her financially.

While her passion continued, Rodin's interest waned after *Muse,* the sculpture for which she was modelling, was complete.

Travel and Transport

BATTLE OF THE WARSHIPS

The Imperial Japanese Navy launched the world's biggest warship, *Satsuma*, with four 12-inch guns but it was overshadowed by the Royal Navy's HMS *Dreadnought*, which sent ripples out around the world.

At a time when battleships usually mounted only four big guns and an array of smaller weapons, *Dreadnought*'s ten 12-inch guns made all other battleships out-of-date.

Powered by new steam turbines she had a top speed of 21 knots, three knots faster than battleships with traditional piston engines.

HMS *Dreadnought* was the largest, fastest, most powerful warship ever seen and navies around the world rushed to match her.

WORLD'S BIGGEST LINER

Britain also ruled the waves when it came to commercial ships. Cunard's *Lusitania*, launched in Glasgow on June 7, was the world's largest and fastest passenger liner.

The liner, and her sister ship *Mauretania*, were constructed with the aid of generous loans from the British government.

Cunard chairman Lord Inverclyde had successfully lobbied the Balfour administration for a loan of £2.6 million for the construction of both ships. In return, they met Admiralty specifications and could be requisitioned in times of war. The government agreed to pay Cunard an annual subsidy of £150,000 for maintaining both ships in a state of war readiness, plus an additional £68,000 to carry Royal Mail.

HMS Dreadnought out-powered all other warships with its 10 x 12in guns. The fastest ship in the world, she further established Britain's ocean-going dominance.

Cunard's Lusitania was the largest and fastest luxury liner but is best remembered as being torpedoed by a German submarine in 1915, killing 1,198 of the 1,959 people on board, the second largest passenger disaster after the Titanic. But, in 1906, her launch was celebrated and she won the Blue Riband in 1907 on her maiden voyage to New York City.

'SILVER GHOST' IS THE ENVY OF THE WORLD

Charles Rolls and Henry Royce founded 'Rolls-Royce Limited' this year and unveiled their newest automobile, the elegant six-cylinder 'Silver Ghost'.

The name was originally a marketing term for a promotional model of a new 40/50hp model, shown at the Olympia Car Show in November. The company's Commercial Managing Director, Claude Johnson, ordered the car to be painted silver with silver-plated fittings. A plaque with the words 'Silver Ghost' adorned the bulkhead. The aim was to raise public awareness of the new company and to show the reliability and quietness of their new car.

The Silver Ghost title was taken up by the press and soon all 40/50s were called by that name.

The quality of the car and the utmost attention to detail secured the company's early reputation. Deliveries commenced the following year.

BAKERLOO LINE OPENS

A new stretch of underground railway opened in London on March 10, from Baker Street to Waterloo.

Originally known as the Baker Street and Waterloo Railway, the name was officially changed in July 1906 to the Bakerloo Railway reflecting the nickname coined by the *Evening News* newspaper. Over 36,000 passengers used it on the day of opening. The Elephant & Castle station opened in August.

THE ARRIVAL OF TRAFFIC NOISE

The popularity of motorised transport was starting to make London a much noisier place. In August, Winston Churchill and 100 other eminent people protested at street noise caused by vehicles.

The police started to apply the licensing law requiring no 'undue noise' with some vigour and by November many London buses were off the road, banned for being too noisy.

London bus companies complained that they were being driven out of business and pointed fingers at powerful lobbyists, not least London County Council, which ran the trams.

A report for the year showed that London buses were involved in 2,448 accidents, many of them attributed to mechanical failure.

Toys

The roaring success of the teddy bear led to the first British bear being made by J.K. Farnell.

Other early bears were made by W.J. Terry, Dean's Rag Book Co Ltd, Chad Valley and Chiltern.

While early British bears copied the German look, they later began to change – their bodies became fatter, their faces flatter and their arms and legs shorter. British makers also experimented with different materials.

J. K. Farnell was based in Notting Hill, in London. A silk merchant by trade, Farnell originally set up the company in 1840 to make small household items such as pincushions and tea cosies.

After Farnell's death his children, Henry and Agnes, continued the family business and moved to Acton in West London. Here they started to make soft toys using materials such as rabbit skin. They were soon using the more usual mohair and the company eventually produced the first British teddy bear. Such was its success that Farnell quickly established itself as one of the leading manufacturers of teddy bears.

Sport

'INTERIM' OLYMPICS

After the disappointing lack of interest in the Paris and St Louis Games, the Olympics returned to Athens with an 'Interim Games' on April 27, to celebrate the tenth anniversary of the start of the modern era.

King Edward VII and Queen Alexandra joined the Greek Royal Family for the opening ceremony.

The Games were dominated by the French athletes, with the Americans also successful. They attracted huge crowds, who also enjoyed the spectacular shows which included illuminating the Acropolis.

These were the first games at which the British Olympic Association was responsible for financing a Great Britain team. The Association received no government assistance, but in common with other competing nations, they were offered a contribution by the Greek organisers.

The British team, 40 strong, performed well. Lieutenant Henry Hawtrey won gold in the five-mile race. Other golds came from the Irishmen Con Leahy in the High Jump and Peter O'Connor in the Triple Jump.

After the sparse attendances in 1900 and 1904, Athens rekindled the enthusiasm that had launched the Games in 1896.

The eruption of Mount Vesuvius meant that the Italian government asked that the 1908 Games, due to be staged in Rome, be given to another city. London put in a bid which proved to be successful.

FIRST MAJOR GRAND PRIX

The town of Le Mans in France was the home of the first major Grand Prix race on June 27.

The track was laid out on public roads to the east of the city, linking Le Mans with the towns of St Calais and La Ferte Bernard. It was 65 miles in length.

The race, organised by the Automobile Club de France, was held over two days and was won by Ferenc Szisz, a Franco-Hungarian driving a Renault.

BRITISH DOMINATION AT WIMBLEDON

Dorothea Douglass exacted revenge over May Sutton when she regained her Wimbledon crown in the Ladies' Single championships, which she had lost to Sutton the previous year. In a hard fought match, in front of a cheering crowd, Douglass won 6–3, 9–7.

In the men's singles, Lawrence Doherty from the UK won for the fifth time in succession, beating fellow Briton Frank Riseley 6–4, 4–6, 6–2, 6–3.

Afterwards 'Laurie' and his elder brother Reginald, known as 'Reggie', announced their retirement from competitive tennis after dominating the game for a decade.

Reggie won Wimbledon in four successive years from 1897, while Laurie, who lost to his brother in the 1898 final, won every year since 1902. Between them, they won the doubles eight times, and four times secured the Davis Cup for Great Britain.

GORDON BENNETT AIR BALLOON RACE

The first hot-air balloon race took place in Paris on September 30. The event was sponsored by James Gordon Bennett Jr., the millionaire sportsman and owner of the *New York Herald* newspaper. It was named the Gordon Bennett Cup.

The goal of the race – which still continues today – was and is simple: to fly the furthest distance from the launch site.

Sixteen balloons launched from the Tuileries Gardens in Paris, and a huge crowd of 200,000 watched the graceful flights. The race was won by US Army Lieutenant Frank Lahm and his co-pilot Henry Hersey, who flew 402.09 miles, landing in Whitby, Yorkshire.

The Home

MRS BEETON LIVES ON

Mrs Beeton's *Book of Household Management* was a domestic bible for many Victorians, providing recipes, dinner party etiquette and tips on handling domestic staff. Although the lady herself died in

The first hot air balloon race was named after its sponsor, Gordon Bennett and took place in Paris. The first manned balloon ride was in a Montgolfier balloon, piloted by Pilâtre de Rozier in 1783 (see image).

Airship ascent at Ranelagh on 7th July. Chairs were arranged so ladies in their finery could watch the balloon rise.

1865, at the tender age of 28 her book continued to be updated and was again a publishing success in 1906.

The introduction to the edition states: 'In every English speaking country, 'Household Management' has appeared with the wedding presents of a bride as surely as the proverbial salt cellars.'

A fascinating glimpse into past lives, the book includes such delights as stuffed pig's head, recommended as a breakfast dish, and a leek soup made with sheep's head which includes the instructions: 'Prepare the head, either by skinning, or cleaning the skin very nicely; split it in two; take out the brains, and put it into boiling water.'

Advice on shopping is somewhat surprising considering the reader was assumed to have servants. Throughout, the mistress of the house is advised that 'the lady who markets herself (i.e. shops for herself) will end up with the best, that is the cheapest and most seasonal [produce].'

The book also reveals the lengths that the wealthy household went to in the name of entertaining, with a whole chapter on folding serviettes, menus and guest cards and how to make them into miniature swans, ballet shoes and even deckchairs.

The list of groceries in the books not only tells us the relative cost of everyday items but also throws up some surprising additions to the every-day shopping list:

Beef tea in skins	5s to 6s per lb
Blancmange powder	6d per box
Chocolate	10d per lb
Cocoa	2s 6d per lb
Coffee	
Whole or ground	1s to 2s per lb
Mocha	1s 9d per lb
Curry Powder	1s 6d per lb bottle
Fruit – Dried	
Apricots	1s 3d per lb
Lunettes	1s 4d per lb
Melons	1s 6d per lb
Ginger	8d per lb
Isinglass	5d per packet

(A gelling agent made from the swim bladders of fish!)

Mrs Beeton also lists eight types of tea: Congou, Ceylon, Orange Pekoe, Gunpowder, Assam Pekoe, Oolong, Young Hyson and Consolidated. Prices varied between 1s.2d per lb to 3s per lb.

Mrs Beeton's domestic bible was, of course, aimed at the middle and upper classes whose purses could easily stretch to such luxuries. To put those prices in perspective, the average farm labourer would earn 15s. 1d a week.

TIMES THEY ARE A-CHANGING

Two events occurred which were to have no immediate impact on daily life but would bring dramatic change in the future: the washing machine was invented and William S. Kellogg baked his first cornflakes.

Although popular wisdom has it that the first electric washing machine was invented by American Alva Fisher, there is some dispute amongst historians on this point. Fisher invented the 'Thor', a drum-type gadget which was the first electric-powered washing machine to be mass produced. He took it to the Hurley Machine Company of Chicago, Illinois, who introduced it in 1908, and a patent was issued on August 9 1910.

However, US records show that a Louis P. Willsea applied for a patent on his electric washing machine in January 1908. Willsea's 'Centrifugal Machine' was designed for commercial laundries but employed the same basic principles as the type that would be found in homes.

The discovery of cornflakes by Dr William Kellogg was to change the breakfast tables of the Western world forever. A firm believer in the role of diet in a healthy lifestyle, Dr Kellogg started experimenting with cereals in 1894 as a means of feeding psychiatric patients at Battle Creek Sanatorium. Interrupted during his work one day, he left some cooked wheat dough exposed for a day and discovered that, when passed through rollers, it produced a single flake for each wheat berry.

After several more years perfecting his new cereal, Kellogg launched his Cornflakes in 1906. In July, after a full-page ad in the *Ladies' Home Journal*, sales leapt to 2,900 cases a day. A hundred years on, the Kellogg Company is still the world's leading producer of breakfast cereals.

The Changing Role of Women

SUFFRAGETTES CHRISTENED

Three years after the formation of the Women's Social and Political Union, the word 'suffragette' was coined by the *Daily Mail*. Originally intended as a derogatory term for the society's members, it soon became synonymous with the bravery and fortitude of those who fought for women's rights.

THE FIGHT RAGES ON

Fearing a motion by the new Labour leader, James Keir Hardie, would be talked out, a group of women marched on the House of Commons in April. Shouting 'Give us votes!', they halted a debate and waved a white flag emblazoned with the words 'Justice for Women' in the Ladies' Gallery. The police were called and the debate suspended without a vote.

A few weeks later, the new Liberal Prime Minister, Henry Campbell-Bannerman, agreed to meet a delegation from both the WSPU and the National Union of Women's Suffrage Societies. The women, who included Emmeline Pankhurst, Annie Kenney and Emmeline Pethick-Lawrence, were joined by Keir Hardie.

Although the Prime Minister assured them that he was personally in favour of women being given the vote, he claimed his ministers would never agree and advised them against drastic action.

Reminded by Emily Davies, of the NUWSS, that she had handed in a petition some 40 years previously, the PM replied, 'It is more likely you will succeed if you wait than if you act now in a pugnacious spirit.'

A furious Emmeline Pankhurst marched down to Trafalgar Square where she told a waiting crowd of 6,000; 'We have been patient too long. We will be patient no longer.' The result of the meeting was a huge blow to the organisations, which had supported Liberal MPs in the belief that they would be sympathetic when they took office. From that point on, members fielded independent male candidates in elections and withdrew support for the Liberals.

October saw more arrests as suffragettes disrupted the opening of Parliament. Among the 11 jailed were Emmeline's daughters, Adela and Sylvia Pankhurst. On being sentenced another convicted suffragette, Emmeline Pethick-Lawrence, commented, 'Women of England, we are going to prison for you and therefore we do it gladly.'

A month later Keir Hardie introduced a bill on female emancipation to the House of Commons.

Elsewhere, the universal suffrage moved a step closer when Finland became the first European country to grant voting rights to women and all previously excluded men over 24.

NO SPORTING CHANCE

The new trend for hockey, lacrosse and netball in ladies' colleges came under attack from a leading academic in the US. Dr Dudley Sargant, physical director of Harvard University, felt contact sports should be played only by men. 'Let woman rather confine herself to the lighter and more graceful forms of gymnastics and athletics and make herself supreme in those,' he said.

In the UK, Parliament passed a bill banning women from 'dangerous sports' after parachutist Lily Cove died when she jumped from a hot-air balloon at a village event in Haworth.

Science

SONAR INVENTED

In New York, Lewis Nixon, a shipbuilding executive and naval architect, announced the invention of sonar on May 26.

It used transmitted and reflected underwater sound waves to detect and locate submerged objects and to measure their distances underwater. Nixon invented it as a way of detecting

Jolly hockey sticks! Games such as hockey, lacrosse and netball, were deemed too rough for ladies to play.

icebergs but it was a passive listening device that did not send out signals and could not have saved the *Titanic* from striking an iceberg six years later.

NEW TYPE OF TYPEWRITER

Robert Turner of Norfolk was granted a patent for his invention of a typewriter which used an innovative automatic carriage return.

SOS BECOMES INTERNATIONAL DISTRESS SIGNAL

In Berlin, on October 3, the first wireless telegraphy conference agreed to the adoption of SOS as the international distress signal.

PICTURES TRANSMITTED BY TELEGRAPH

A picture was transmitted by telegraph over more than a thousand miles by German professor Arthur Korn on October 17.

Korn built on an existing invention, by Italian physicist Luigi Cerebotani, for taking a photograph a small part at a time and producing, from each part, an electrical current corresponding to its shade of grey.

The invention paved the way for newspapers being able to publish pictures taken only hours before on the other side of the Atlantic.

WIRELESS BREAKTHROUGH

American scientist Lee De Forest was responsible for a major development in wireless with his invention of the triode valve.

The triode consisted of three elements, sealed in a vacuum into a device like an electric light bulb. It amplified, without distortion, the feeble electric currents in wireless equipment. It led the way for more powerful transmitters and the detection of weaker signals, as well as communication over longer distances.

Chapter Eight

1907

Politics

NO TO CHANNEL TUNNEL

THE PRIME Minister, Sir Henry Campbell-Bannerman, expressed Government opposition to the Channel Tunnel Bill. The plan, to construct a railway tunnel under the English Channel, was also opposed by The War Office, who feared it was a threat to the nation's defences. The bill was later withdrawn.

COURT OF APPEAL

The Court of Criminal Appeal was created in the UK to replace the Court for Crown Cases Reserved. The new court was empowered to quash convictions that rested on errors of fact or of law.

RUSSIAN PARLIAMENT FASHIONED TO FIT

Fledgling Russian parliament, the Duma, continued to have a turbulent time. Having dissolved the first Duma last year for its unacceptable demands for reform, Tsar Nicholas II was hoping for more moderate representatives the second time around.

After a new round of elections, the second Duma convened in February but, after further clashes, the Prime Minister (and Tsar's ally) Peter Stolypin eventually accused 55 socialist deputies of plotting against the monarchy. And the Tsar once again closed down the Duma on June 16.

As plans for a third Duma were drawn up, Stolypin made crucial changes to the electoral law, which led to a more conservative representative.

National minorities were excluded and the number of people who could vote in Poland, Siberia, the Caucasus and in Central Asia was dramatically reduced. The new electoral law also gave better representation to the nobility and gave greater power to the large landowners to the detriment of the peasants. Those owning their own homes elected over half the urban deputies.

The third Duma met on 14th November, 1907. The former coalition of Socialist-Revolutionaries, Mensheviks, Bolsheviks, Octobrists and the Constitutional Democrat Party was now outnumbered by the reactionaries and the nationalists. Unlike the previous Dumas, this one ran its full-term of five years.

PREMIER OF BULGARIA SHOT DEAD

Bulgarian Prime Minister Dimitar Petkov was assassinated on February 26 by an anarchist. He was shot in broad daylight in the centre of Sofia. Petkov had been PM for just four months. He was succeeded by Petar Gudev.

NEW ZEALAND GAINS 'INDEPENDENCE'

New Zealand gained autonomy from the UK as a dominion within the British Empire. Crowds cheered as NZ Prime Minister, Sir Joseph Ward, read the proclamation of dominion status from the steps of Parliament on September 26.

In a rousing speech he said that the move from colony to dominion marked an important symbolic shift in New Zealand's perceptions of nationhood. This would, he hoped, remind the world that New Zealand was an important player in its own right.

Royalty

NEW SHAH OF PERSIA CROWNED

Mohammad Ali Mirza was crowned Shah of Persia in a colourful ceremony at the Royal Palace in Tehran on January 19.

According to ancient custom, the royal procession entered the throne room one hour after midday. It was led by the younger brother of the new Shah, followed by priests, mullahs and dignitaries, with the new monarch at the end.

As the Shah took his seat on the Peacock Throne – richly adorned with emeralds – the crowning ceremony took place. Afterwards the Shah descended from the throne and walked in front of the foreign delegates, stopping to say a few words to each. The British representative, Cecil Spring-Rice, communicated the contents of a telegram received that morning from King Edward wishing the Shah a long and prosperous reign.

'IRISH CROWN JEWELS' STOLEN

This was the year of the theft of the so-called 'Irish Crown Jewels' – the name given to the Sovereign's personal insignia as a knight of the Most Illustrious Order of St Patrick.

Yhey were stolen from Dublin Castle in July, shortly before a visit by King Edward VII. Their fate remains unknown to this day.

The Most Illustrious Order of Saint Patrick was created in 1783 by George III, to reward those in high office in Ireland and Irish peers on whose support the government of the day depended. It served as the national Order of Ireland as the Garter was for England and the Thistle for Scotland.

Edward VII with the Prince of Wales, the future George V.

In 1830 the Crown Jewellers, Rundell & Bridge, created the regalia from jewels that had belonged to Queen Charlotte, the consort of George III.

There were two principal pieces – the star and the badge. The eight-pointed star consisted mostly of Brazilian diamonds. In the centre, a shamrock of emeralds shone from the heart of a ruby cross which lay upon a background of blue enamel. Encircling this central motif was the motto of the order, *Quis Separabit?* (who can separate us?) and the date MDCCLXXIII (1783) all in rose diamonds.

The badge was of similar splendour, with its shamrock of emeralds on

A fascinating glimpse into the extent of the royal family which encompasses the whole of European royalty, 24 in total.
Those featured include the child Prince Olaf of Norway, Edward VII, the Queen of Portugal (black dress, white-topped hat), Grand Duchess Vladimir of Russia, the Queen of Spain, the Queen of Norway (2nd from left, standing), Kaiser Wilhelm, the Princess of Wales (later Queen Mary), the King of Spain (in the middle of the back row, wearing a tie), the Empress of Germany (next to him) and Queen Alexandra (standing between a gap in the chairs).

Taken by William Downey, the Court photographer at Windsor in November. He used an arc lamp of 10,000 candlepower because of failing light. (Image courtesy of the Estate of Stanley Shoop).

a ruby cross surrounded by a blue enamel band bearing the motto and date in rose diamonds. This was enclosed in an outer circle of large Brazilian diamonds, the whole being surrounded by a harp and loop framed in diamonds.

They were kept in the strongroom of Dublin Castle under the custody of the Ulster King of Arms, the Principal Herald of Ireland, and his assistants.

Prior to the arrival of King Edward and Queen Alexandra, for the purpose of investing Lord Castletown with the Order of St. Patrick, it was discovered that the jewels had been stolen. They were estimated to be worth about £40,000 in 1907.

The public amazement over the theft was nothing compared with the official consternation. An investigation into the disappearance was carried out but the thief or the whereabouts of the jewels have never been discovered.

Historical Events

KINGSTON DESTROYED BY EARTHQUAKE

A huge earthquake in Jamaica on January 14 devastated the capital of Kingston, destroying most of the buildings and killing over 800 people. Hundreds more were trapped under the rubble or badly injured. The hospitals were unable to cope with the crisis and a fire blazed through the streets for four days.

Rampant looting broke out and armed guards had to be posted throughout the city.

England, America and Cuba sent ships laden with provisions, extra surgeons and soldiers.

Under Governor Olivier's guidance, a new city rose from the ruins. The main public buildings on King Street and the public gardens, as well as several new roads, were built along a basic grid system. Olivier's determination and enthusiasm kept him in office until 1913.

RIOTS IN KOREA AS EMPEROR OUSTED

Japan tightened its iron grip over Korea after the Korean Emperor complained about the injustice of the dominant power's presence.

The previous autumn, Emperor Kojong had sent three representatives on his behalf to the Second International Conference on Peace at The Hague to protest against Japan's 1905 protectorate agreement over Korea.

But his appeal was shunned by the delegates who had been sent from 43 countries to discuss world peace.

In retaliation for Kojong's protest, Japan pushed through a new agreement, considerably increasing its powers in Korea. The Japanese resident general in Seoul, Marquis Ito, now had total control over all local administration, including the appointment of high officials. He also took the opportunity to recruit Japanese personnel to positions of authority, and reorganised the courts of justice.

The new Japan-Korea Convention was signed in July, 1907 but rioting broke out when the Emperor was forced to abdicate in place of his son, Emperor Sunjong, who was more pliable to Japan's wishes.

The rioting was harshly suppressed and ringleaders executed, which only increased Korean hatred of the Japanese for their occupation.

Social Change

SCOUTING FOR BOYS

Sir Robert Baden-Powell, a hero of the siege of Mafeking, had long been considering ways to get boys to engage in healthy outdoor activity. His concern had arisen when he saw the poor health of the young men who had turned up to enrol in the army during the Boer War, many of whom had to be turned away.

His experience of army scouts during the campaigns in India and Africa led him to think that the benefits and values of military life could be instilled at a younger age.

In 1906, he had circulated a memorandum called *Boy Scouts: A Suggestion* in which he outlined plans to set up an organisation to encourage discipline, survival skills, camaraderie and good citizenship.

The response from politicians and public figures was positive, and on July 25, 20 lads from all walks of life sailed across Poole Harbour to Brownsea Island where they set up camp and learned such skills as woodcraft, tracking and first aid. At night they gathered at the camp fire to hear stories of Baden-Powell's adventures abroad.

The Scout movement was born and in 1908 Baden-Powell outlined his principles in the handbook *Scouting for Boys*. The groups were designed to stop the rise of 'shirkers' in every area of society. Modern day living and city squalor had, he believed, produced 'thousands of boys and young men, pale narrow-chested, hunched up, miserable specimens, smoking endless cigarettes'.

By 1910, the Scout movement had 108,000 members.

FIRST MONTESSORI SCHOOL

Maria Montessori opened her first school in Rome and revolutionised education for the under-fives. The progressive Italian doctor believed that each child has a unique potential and that their individual talents should be encouraged to surface.

Formerly an expert in children with special needs, she was given the chance to study 50 poor children from the slum of St Lorenzo. The reputation of her *Casa dei Bambino* (House of Children) spread far and wide and led, eventually, to her methods being adopted in the States, the UK, India and many other countries.

In the UK, medical tests were provided in schools for the first time and appropriate treatment for illness given free.

Fashion

LUCILE AND THE MERRY WIDOW

London's leading female fashion designer, Lucile, otherwise known as Lady Duff-Gordon, revolutionised headwear when she designed the 'Merry Widow' hat. The wide-brimmed hat, decorated with sumptuous silk and showy feathers, was part of the costume design for a new play *The Merry Widow,* starring Lily Elsie.

The play, and the hat, were a huge success and Lucile's fame spread. 'The triumph of *The Merry Widow* was also a triumph for me,' said Lady Duff-Gordon in her autobiography. *The Merry Widow* hat brought in a fashion which carried the name of Lucile, its creator, all over Europe and the States. The trend for unfeasibly tall hats was over as wide-brimmed hats, decorated with feathers, ribbons and fabric flowers, particularly cabbage roses, became the must-have fashion item.

THE BRA IN VOGUE

Bust bodices and bust improvers had been increasingly favoured over the more restrictive corset since the 1880s, but the term 'brassiere' was first coined in 1907 in *American Vogue.*

In fact, brassieres or similar garments had been worn by various

Brassieres came into fashion when *American Vogue* used the term.

civilisations for 3,000 years. Romans wore a band of fabric to restrict their breasts, while the ancient Greeks preferred to accentuate their bosoms by tying a belt underneath their breasts. The more liberated Minoans, however, wore cloth garments to both enhance and reveal their assets.

In fact, the term brassiere, meaning 'arm support', was being used by manufacturers as early as 1904 but the mention in *American Vogue* put the word on the map and resulted in its inclusion in the 1911 edition of the Oxford English Dictionary.

SWEAT SHOP COMMITTEE

Following the successful Anti-Sweating exhibition of the previous year, the issue of sweated labour and low pay for homeworkers entered the debating chamber of the House of Commons. In 1907 after lengthy discussions, a Select Committee was set up to investigate the plight of homeworkers in the clothing industry.

CHEMICAL COLOUR

A year after the advent of the perm, another new product was to revolutionise the hair styles of the future. French chemist Eugene Schueller came up with a formula for synthetic hair dye by modifying the ingredients used for fabric dye.

His new range of dyes, in gold red and dark shades, was called 'Auréole' and would form the foundation of the hugely successful cosmetic firm, L'Oréal. It was also the starting point for the entire hair dye industry.

Entertainment

FILM

The pioneering Lumière brothers launched a new process which would change the future of colour photography. The process, named Autochrome Lumière, involved taking three scenes through the primary colours – red, yellow and blue. The three negatives were then covered with sheets made from microscopic dots and a light shone from behind to produce a colour image.

At the same time, another innovative film-maker and founder of Universal Studios, Carl Laemmle, was attempting to create sound for films using phonographs. The experiments resulted in a process called 'Syncroscope', which was demonstrated a few times before it was dropped.

Russian-born scrap dealer Louis B. Mayer took over The Gem Theatre, a rundown burlesque venue in Haverhill, Massachusetts, in order to turn it into a picture house. On November 18, it reopened as The Orpheum. Despite being Jewish, Mayer chose a Christian film for the opening, to disassociate the theatre from its racy past. The success of The Orpheum led to a takeover of four more theatres in the district and a further expansion put him in control of New England's largest theatre chain.

In 1916, Mayer formed his first production company and, eight years later, he joined forced with Marcus Loew, owner of Metro Pictures and Goldwyn Pictures, to form Metro-Goldwyn-Mayer. As the effective head of MGM, Louis was one of the most influential figureheads in Twentieth Century cinema and was the creator of the 'star system' within the studio.

Five years after setting up his own studio, British cinema pioneer Will Barker bought his first sound stage and moved his entire operation from North London to West London. Ealing Studios was born and was set to establish Britain's place in film-making history with such classics as *Passport to Pimlico, The Blue Lamp* and *The Ladykillers*.

Europe released its first full-length feature film, *L'Enfant Prodigue (The Prodigal Son)*. The 90-minute film, directed by Michel Carré from his own three-act play, premiered at a Paris theatre on June 20.

Other films released this year included the first screen adaptation of Jules Verne's novel *20,000 Lieues Sous les Mers (20,000 Leagues Under the Sea)* and the first-ever *Ben-Hur*, made without the permission of author Lew Wallace. The subsequent successful court case by publisher Harper and Brothers, against Kalem Studios, was a landmark in copyright law.

US showbusiness magazine *Variety* began publishing film reviews for the first time in January, two years after its formation.

THEATRE

Inspired by the spectacular *Folies Bergères* show in Paris, impresario Florenz Ziegfeld conceived an elaborate Broadway production along the same lines, as a showcase for his wife, entertainer Anna Held. *The Ziegfeld Follies* opened on July 18, 1907, at New York's Jardin de Paris.

The concept was to survive 30 years, continuing even after Ziegfeld's death in 1934, and over the years would include such entertainers as W.C.Fields, Eddie Cantor, The Tiller Girls and Fanny Brice.

In ballet, Russian ballerina Anna Pavlova introduced the *Dying Swan* solo, choreographed for her by Michael Fokine. It was to become her most famous solo.

In London, a long-brewing row between music hall artists, stage hands and their employers finally boiled over at the Holborn Empire. The theatre's staff walked out on January 22, sparking a strike in most London halls and many suburban venues, organised by the Variety Artists Federation. The 'Music Hall War', over the low pay received by all but the biggest stars, was supported by such luminaries as Marie Dainton, Arthur Roberts and Marie Lloyd.

Marie Lloyd explained her own support for the cause:

'We (the stars) can dictate our own terms. We are fighting not for ourselves, but for the poorer members of the profession, earning thirty shillings to £3 a week. For this they have to do double turns, and now matinées have been added as well. These poor things have been compelled to submit to unfair terms of employment, and I mean to back up the federation in whatever steps are taken.'

The dispute ended in February with an agreement which included a minimum wage and a maximum working week for musicians.

Leading actress, Sarah Bernhardt's autobiography was published in book form, having previously been serialised in *The Strand Magazine*.

MUSIC

Israel Baline, a singing waiter at Pelham's café in New York, had his first song published. *Marie of Sunny Italy* proved popular with the customers and Israel was paid 37 cents by music company Stern.

Legend has it that a printing error led to the young singer being named as Irving Berlin on the cover. Not wanting to tempt fate, he decided the name should stay. He went on to write over 3,000 songs, including the classics *I'm Dreaming of a White Christmas, There's no Business like Showbusiness* and *Puttin' on the Ritz.*

Norwegian composer Edvard Hagerup Grieg died in Bergen on September 4, at the age of 64. He was best known for his *Piano Concerto in A Minor* and the music he composed for Henrik Ibsen's *Peer Gynt.*

Enrico Caruso's recording of *Vesti la Giubba* from Leoncavallo's *Pagliacci* became the first gramophone record to sell a million copies.

Hits of the year included *Bon Bon Buddy* by Alex Rogers, *Honey Boy* by Jack Norworth and *School Days* by Will D.Cobb.

BIRTHS

February 15 – Cesar Romero, Cuban-American actor.
February 17 – Buster Crabbe, American swimmer and actor.
March 11 – Jessie Matthews, British actress and singer.
May 12 – Katherine Hepburn, US Actress.
May 22 – Laurence Olivier, British actor.
May 26 – John Wayne, US actor.
July 16 – Barbara Stanwyck, US actress.
September 15 – Fay Wray, US actress.
September 29 – Gene Autrey, US actor.
October 9 – Jacques Tati, French film director.
December 22 – Peggy Ashcroft, British actress.
December 25 – Cab Calloway, US jazz singer.

DEATHS

September 4 – Edvard Grieg, Norwegian composer.
September 5 – Adolf Østbye, first Norwegian recording artist.

Literature

KIPLING HONOURED

Rudyard Kipling became the first British recipient of the Nobel Prize for Literature. Born and raised in India, to English parents, Kipling had begun his career as a poet and reporter, but had found fame with his short stories, such as *Plain Tales from the Hills*.

His children's classic, *The Jungle Book*, was published in 1894, five years

American author and humorist, Mark Twain, visited Britain and, in an interview with Edgar Wallace, revealed that he was going to the Oxford Pageant – for tips on planning his own funeral – which took place three years later.

after his return to England. Now his best known work, the story of a 'man cub' raised by wild animals has inspired numerous films, including the Walt Disney classic. In 1895 Kipling followed this with *The Second Jungle Book* and, in 1902, *The Just So Stories*.

The adult novel *Kim*, published in 1901, was seen as the definitive novel of life in Imperial India and received huge critical acclaim.

Despite Kipling's previous refusal to accept awards, including the post of Poet Laureate, he was awarded the Nobel Prize on December 10, 'in consideration of the power of observation, originality of imagination, virility of ideas and remarkable talent for narration which characterize the creations of this world-famous author'.

THE PLAY'S A RIOT

J.M. Synge published his controversial work *The Playboy of the Western World* which debuted at W.B.Yeats' Abbey Theatre in Dublin. Many Irish people were offended by the play, in which a young man appears in an Irish village saying that he has killed his own father. Rather than condemning him, the villagers rally round and enjoy his story.

Anger at the questionable morals of the characters caused riots in the streets and the playgoers were arrested. Political party Sinn Fein called the work 'aA vile and inhuman story told in the foulest language'.

BIRTHS

February 3 – James A. Michener, US novelist and Pulitzer Prize winner.
February 21 – W. H. Auden, British poet.
May 12 – Leslie Charteris, British novelist and creator of *The Saint*.
May 13 – Daphne du Maurier, British novelist.
May 22 – George Remi, alias Herge, Belgian creator of *Tintin*.
December 10 – Rumer Godden, British novelist.

Architecture

JUSTICE IS DONE

Five years after construction began, the new Criminal Courts of Justice were completed.

Londoners lined the route on February 27 as King Edward VII and Queen Alexandra were driven through flower-lined streets to the Old Bailey to open the building.

Built on the site of the notorious Newgate Prison, the imposing structure, designed by E.W. Mountford, is topped by a statue of Lady Justice by F.W. Pomeroy. Standing on the impressive dome, Lady Justice carries a sword and a pair of scales to represent justice and equality.

Above the door the inscription reads 'Defend the Children of the Poor and Punish the Wrongdoer'.

Occupying the site of the main Roman West Gate to the ancient City of London, now called the Square Mile, the Old Bailey had to be partially rebuilt in the 1950s after extensive damage was sustained in the Blitz.

In New York, the Singer Building, still under construction in 1907, became the tallest in the world.

GERMAN LANDMARK

The world renowned architect Hermann Muthesius, author of *The English House*, set up the influential group *the Deutscher Werkbund*. The idea behind the association of German architects, designers and industrialists was to create links between arts, crafts and mass market production, bringing Germany in line with international competitors, including the UK and the US.

Original members were 12 architects, including Theodor Fischer and Josef Hoffman, and 12 manufacturing companies.

In 1914, the Werkbund were instrumental in the successful Cologne Exhibition and commissioned a magnificent theatre to be built for the event. Sadly, the building was destroyed in World War Two after standing for just a year.

BIRTHS

June 17 – Charles Eames, US designer.
August 13 – Basil Spence, Scottish architect of Coventry Cathedral.
December 15 – Oscar Niemeyer, Brazilian architect and pioneer of reinforced concrete.

Art

CUBISM COMETH

Pablo Picasso's work *Les Demoiselles d'Avignon* caused huge controversy in the art world. The skewed perspective and strange angular features of the five nudes were a radical departure from previous styles and some even believed that the artist meant it as a joke.

The work is heavily influenced by the paintings of Paul Cezanne and the growing interest in African art.

The new distorted art form was developed over the next few years by Picasso and Braque in Montmatre, Paris, and by Spanish artist Juan Gris, who worked with Picasso from 1908 until the outbreak of war in 1914.

Although Cubism as a movement is said to have started in 1908, when the term was coined by critic Louis Vauxcelles in an article about a work by Braque, *Les Demoiselles* is often cited as the beginning of the first phase, now known as protocubism.

Cubists often depict all the surfaces of the subject matter as if they were flattened out so that, for example, every aspect of the face is visible at the same time. Picasso's revolutionary works at this time sought to establish that art may exist without having any relation to reality.

GOLDEN YEAR FOR GUSTAV

Gustav Klimt had a bumper year, producing four of the most popular paintings of his 'Golden Phase', including *The Kiss* and the first *Portrait of Adele Bloch-Bauer*. The Austrian artist's work at this time was frequently embossed with gold leaf and was well received by critics and public alike.

The Kiss, which shows a couple embracing, shrouded in gold, was to become one of his most famous works while the portrait of the Viennese socialite, the first of two, sold for a record $135 million (£73 million) in New York in 2006.

On her death in 1925, Adele Bloch-Bauer bequeathed the Klimt masterpieces to the Austrian State Gallery. However, they were stolen by the Nazis in World War Two when her widowed husband was forced to flee their home. Returned to the family in 2006, the first portrait was sold by Adele's niece, Maria Altman, and bought by Estee Lauder heir Ronald S. Lauder for his Neue Galerie in New York.

Other paintings this year included Claude Monet's *Water Lilies Giverny no. 3* and Henri Rousseau's *The Snake Charmer*.

Travel and Transport

ATLANTIC CROSSING IN RECORD TIME

The new Cunard turbine liner, *Lusitania*, launched last year, sailed on her maiden voyage to New York City in a record speed of just under five days, taking back the Blue Riband for Britain.

WORLD'S FIRST WORKING HELICOPTER

Frenchman Paul Cornu, a bicycle maker and engineer, invented the world's first working helicopter. Powered by two motor-driven propellers above the pilot, it lifted vertically off the ground for about a foot in height, carrying a passenger, for 20 seconds, on November 13.

Although Cornu paid much attention to the control of the aircraft, it proved to be quite ineffective and impractical and it was abandoned after a few flights.

BRITANNIA RULES THE WAVES

The world's largest battle cruiser, HMS *Indomitable*, was launched in Glasgow on March 16.

Like HMS *Dreadnought* before her, *Indomitable* was the first of her kind and effectively turned every other large cruiser obsolete. At this point in history it seemed that Britain really did rule the waves.

BRITISH AIRSHIP GETS LIFT-OFF

Britain's first military airship, the '*Nulli Secundus*' (Latin: 'Second to none'), took to the skies on September 10.

Designed by Col. John Capper of the Royal Engineers and Samuel Cody, she was built at the Government's balloon factory at Farnborough, Kent. On 10 October, she was moored at Crystal Palace to avoid damage in high winds when a shower of rain caused damage to the delicate skin of her envelope, causing it to split open and the airship to crash. The remains were taken back to Farnborough where they were used in the manufacture of *Nulli Secundus II*.

FIRST LONDON TAXICABS

The first taxicabs started operating in London. The name derived from the compulsory fitting of taximeters inside the cabs, which measured the distance travelled – or time taken – thus allowing an accurate fare to be determined.

Toys

MECCANO BUILDS A REPUTATION

Frank Hornby's 'Mechanics Made Easy' set had a name change to Meccano. The set consisted of metal strips and plates, with nuts and bolts, a spanner and screwdriver. The early sets came in tin boxes and the parts were unpainted metal. Rods, wheels, pulleys and gears were later added.

The first taxi cabs were hailed, replacing the horse-drawn Hansom cabs, designed by Joseph Hansom in 1834.

MARCH OF THE TEDDY BEAR

The popularity for teddy bears continued to increase around the world, with more and more toy manufacturers starting to produce them.

In Germany, Johann Hermann persuaded his family to join him in making teddy bears and his children later set up teddy bear companies of their own.

Teddy bears were at the top of many British children's Christmas wish list and Steiff declared 1907 as The Year of the Bear.

Germany was still dominant in toy production of all kind but William Britain, who had founded 'Britains' in the UK in 1860, had developed a new method of hollow-casting lead soldiers which meant that they were lighter and cheaper in comparison to the German solid lead models. He gained a stronghold on the market and the central London department store, Gamage's in Holborn, took up these new figures and sold them at discounted prices. Britains became a limited company on the 4 December 1907.

Sport

HISTORY MADE AT WIMBLEDON

History was made in the Men's Singles Championship at Wimbledon when the title went abroad for the first time.

Norman Brookes of Australia beat Britain's Arthur Gore 6–4, 6–2, 6–2. Brookes underlined his prowess by winning the doubles at Wimbledon with New Zealander Anthony Wilding. Brookes was also part of an Australasian team which broke Britain's four-year hold on the Davis Cup this year, when they won 3–2.

In the Ladies' final at Wimbledon, Britain's Dorothea Douglass faced America's May Sutton for the third time in a row, with Sutton reclaiming the title with a 6–1, 6–4 victory.

THE OPEN TITLE GOES ABROAD

In golf, Arnaud Massy of France became the first overseas player to win The Open.

His victory raised the profile of the game in France and, with three other major players, Massy put on exhibition matches, in various European cities, that contributed significantly to the increased popularity of golf on the continent.

Massy had caddied for top players at Biarritz and moved to Berwick, Scotland, when he was 21 to learn more about the game. He married a local girl and entered several Open Championships where he gained first rate experience before eventually claiming the title at Hoylake, Liverpool, in 1907.

During the championship, his wife gave birth to a daughter, and he cut short his celebrations to return to Berwick. He was greeted at the railway station by a large cheering crowd. They christened the baby Hoylake after his triumph.

SEEDS SOWN FOR HOME OF ENGLISH RUGBY

A 10-acre market garden, 12 miles from the centre of London, was purchased for £5,572.12s.6d as a home for English Rugby.

Bought by Billy Williams, a Rugby Football Union (RFU) committee member, it became known as 'Billy's cabbage patch' since the site was previously used to grow cabbages and other vegetables, along with fruit trees and mushrooms.

Williams, a former fullback for Harlequins, Middlesex, and London, and who was later an international referee, went to see the Mann family about purchasing their orchard which had been put on the market. He recommended the land to the RFU as an excellent place to build a rugby ground.

Many committee members were against the idea, thinking it too far from London, liable to flooding and too costly, leaving insufficient money for development. But the businessman and RFU treasurer, William Cail, told the RFU to buy it and arranged a £6,000 overdraft at the bank to go with the money they had. Although they spent more than £10,000 in the year after they purchased the land, now known as Twickenham Stadium, it proved to be a fine investment which soon made healthy profits. The first game, between Harlequins and Richmond, took place in 1909 and the first international, England v. Wales, in 1910.

ROYAL HORSE SHOW BEGINS IN LONDON

The first Royal International Horse Show was held at London Olympia. Most participants were of a military background; showing and driving dominated the show schedule. The judging decisions were arbitrary – some marked according to severity of obstacle others on style.

The event was instigated by the Institute of the Horse and Pony Club, the forerunner to the British Horse Society, and quickly became a part of the 'society season'.

The first ever FA Cup final photograph shows Everton's Walter Abbot heading the ball towards the Sheffield goal in the Everton-Sheffield Wednesday match at Crystal

BIRTHS

January 22 – William 'Dixie' Dean, England and Everton footballer.

The Home

A HAVEN IN SUBURBIA

Following the establishment of the first Garden City at Letchworth, the idea of affordable, attractive houses and gardens close to the workplace, first laid out in Ebenezer Howard's 1898 book *Tomorrow,* spread to London.

Hampstead Garden Suburb was to lead the way in the development and design of London suburbs built thereafter. On news of a new underground station in this picturesque area, heiress turned social worker Dame Henrietta Barnett set up a group to save 80 acres from the 'rows of ugly villas such as disfigure Willesden and most of the suburbs of London'. She also set up charitable trusts to buy a further 243 acres from Eton College.

She then joined forces with Letchworth's planners, Sir Raymond Unwin and Barry Parker, to come up with a suburb where all classes of society could find a haven. Sir Raymond was keen 'to do something to meet the housing problem by putting within the reach of the working people the opportunity of taking a cottage with a garden within a 2d. fare of Central London'.

In order to overcome strict by-laws, the Hampstead Garden Suburb Trust promoted a private bill which was to become the cornerstone of town planning in the future. The Hampstead Garden Suburb Act, passed in 1906, stated that building was limited to eight properties per acre, 50 feet apart and the roads at least 40 feet wide. Green spaces, such as woods and heath-lands, were free to all residents and lower ground rents were to be paid on some properties so that workers on low wages could afford them.

Hampstead Garden Suburb was finally founded in 1907 and its designer, Sir Raymond Unwin, was to live there for the remainder of his life.

LIVING ON A SHOESTRING

Eleanor Rathbone, secretary of the Women's Industrial Council in Liverpool, embarked on a study of household expenditure among the city's working-class families. In *How the Casual Labourer Lives*, she modestly claimed that her studies had 'yielded no absolutely new fact of importance', but the 40 households she studied did provide an insight into everyday life in a poor household.

As many of the accounts were long term, lasting up to 62 weeks, they showed the real cost of more expensive items, such as clothing, that were not bought each week.

In 40 per cent of households, the wives worked as well as their husbands, with many taking jobs cleaning, washing or sewing, and others took lodgers to make ends meet. They were also reliant on borrowing and using credit when a 'lumpy' expenditure, such as clothing and shoes, was necessary. Rent varied wildly from region to region, and was a huge consideration in how the rest of the household income could be spent.

The Changing Role of Women

STORMY WEATHER

The National Union of Women's Suffrage Societies organised its first national protest in February, but failed to take the weather into account. Conditions were so poor for the open-air demonstration that it was dubbed 'The Mud March', but the suffragettes were undaunted as ever.

Over 3,000 women from all over the country turned out, making it, at the time, the biggest ever open-air demonstration.

CHRISTABEL'S FRUSTRATION

Christabel Pankhurst passed her law degree at the University of Manchester but, as a woman, was barred from seeking a career as a barrister. After a series of disagreements with her sister Sylvia, who favoured universal suffrage rather than votes for wealthy women only, Christabel moved to London where she took over the Women's Social and Political Union (WSPU).

Emmeline, Christabel's mother and the founder of the movement, also moved to London to concentrate her increasingly militant activities there. However, the two women's domination of the organisation upset many of the members, who believed they made too many decisions without consulting others. Teresa Billington-Grieg, Charlotte Despard and some 70 other members left to form the Women's Freedom League. Although they were militant, they also believed in non-violent demonstration, such as refusing to pay taxes, rather than the campaign of vandalism that the WSPU would soon embark on.

Later in the year, Keir Hardie's Women's Enfranchisement Bill was defeated in Parliament but there was a small victory for the suffragettes when another bill, the Qualification of Women Act, meant that women could be voted onto borough and county councils and could even be elected as mayor.

WSPU supporters Emmeline and Frederick Pethick-Lawrence launched the journal *Votes for Women*.

WOMEN ON THE FRONT LINE

The First Aid Nursing Yeomanry (FANY) was founded to provide first aid to the front line and in field hospitals. The voluntary organisation, re-christened The Princess Royal's Volunteer Corps in 1999, was an invaluable help during the First and Second World Wars, taking on roles as drivers, signallers and coders as well as manning hospitals.

Still going strong today, members provide assistance to civil and military authorities in times of emergency, such as the London bombings in 2007 and the Iraq war.

Nurse Florence Nightingale became the first woman to be awarded the Order of Merit.

Science

FIRST TRANSATLANTIC WIRELESS SERVICE

Guglielmo Marconi perfected his transatlantic wireless system, enabling him to set up a commercial service between Nova Scotia, Canada, and Clifden, Ireland.

HOOVER CLEANS UP

Various forms of vacuum cleaners were on the market but it was James Spangler who invented the first practical, portable, electric version, which remains the basic model today.

Spangler, a janitor in a department store in Ohio, was an asthmatic who wanted to limit the amount of dust he inhaled. He started experimenting and eventually came up with a contraption that incorporated an old motor attached to a soap box which was stapled to a broom handle.

Using a pillow case as a dust collector, Spangler invented a portable, electric vacuum cleaner.

Spangler improved his basic model, the first to use both a cloth filter bag and cleaning attachments, and received a patent in 1908, forming the Electric Suction Sweeper Company.

One of his first buyers was a cousin, whose husband, William H. Hoover, owned the Hoover Harness and Leather Goods Factory. Spangler sold his idea to him and became a partner in the Hoover Electric Suction Sweeper Company.

The company's first produced vacuum was the 'Model O'. It was a great success and spawned many competitors, eager to capitalise on this wonderful new device which transformed cleaning for ever.

Chapter Nine

1908

Politics

NEW LEADERS OF SUPERPOWERS

THE YEAR saw new leaders elected in Britain and the US. Following ill-health, Sir Henry-Campbell-Bannerman resigned and the Chancellor of the Exchequer, Herbert Henry Asquith, became the new Prime Minister on April 12.

Yorkshire-born Asquith – known as 'H.H.' – was a barrister who was elected to Parliament in 1886 as the Liberal representative for East Fife. He achieved his first significant post in 1892 when he became Home Secretary under Gladstone and later under Rosebery.

Campbell-Bannerman gave him the nickname of 'the sledge-hammer' for his forceful and impressive debating skills.

The changeover at 10 Downing Street had been anticipated for some time. Asquith had to travel to Biarritz to be officially received by the King who was holidaying there.

New appointments in the government included David Lloyd George as Chancellor of the Exchequer and Winston Churchill as President of the Board of Trade.

Asquith was a strong believer in free trade, home rule for Ireland and social reform, all vital issues of the day. Campbell-Bannerman died at the age of 71 on April 22.

In the US, Republican candidate William Howard Taft was elected as the country's 27th President on November 3.

After serving for nearly two full terms, the popular Theodore Roosevelt refused to run in the election of 1908 and backed his friend Taft for the presidency.

Taft had served as the Solicitor General of the United States, a federal judge, Governor-General of the Philippines and Secretary of War.

A staunch advocate of world peace, he was a pioneer in international

The Liberal Herbert Henry Asquith ('HH', as he was known) became Prime Minister in April.

arbitration. He fell out with Roosevelt in 1911 when Roosevelt accused him of being too reactionary.

Taft defeated Roosevelt for the Republican nomination in a bruising battle in 1912 and remained President until 1913.

BIRTHS

August 27 – Lyndon Baines Johnson, US President 1963–68.

David Lloyd George was made Chancellor of the Exchequer and would work to undermine Asquith before replacing him as Prime Minister in 1916.

Royalty

ROYAL ASSASSINATION

King Carlos I of Portugal and Crown Prince Luís were assassinated by Republican revolutionaries in Lisbon on February 1.

On their way to the royal palace the carriage, containing King Carlos, Queen Amelia and their sons Luís Filipe and Manuel, drove through central Lisbon. Shots were fired from the crowd by at least two men – Alfredo Costa and Manuel Buiça. The King died immediately, his heir Luís Filipe was mortally wounded, and Prince Manuel was hit in the arm.

The assassins were shot on the spot by royal bodyguards and later recognised as members of the Republican Party. About 20 minutes later,

The Republican William Howard Taft became the 27th President of the US in November when President Theodore 'Teddy' Roosevelt stepped aside for his friend, refusing to stand for office again so Taft could replace him as the Republican candidate.

Prince Luís Filipe died and 19-year old Manuel was acclaimed King of Portugal.

King Carlos was an intelligent and articulate man but he made a great many enemies after he had appointed João Franco as Prime Minister in 1906. Facing Republican dissent, Franco established an authoritarian government in 1907 and ran the country as a dictatorship. But two days after the killings, Franco and his cabinet, facing hostile pressure, resigned. The new King promised to uphold the Constitution, ending his father's repressive regime.

There was also an assassination attempt on the Shah of Persia, Mohammad Ali Mirza, in Tehran on February 28. But he was unscathed and, in July, the liberal Shah decided to reform the Persian parliament along the lines of the Russian Duma.

RUSSIA VISIT IS HOT POTATO FOR KING EDWARD

King Edward made his first visit to Russia on June 9 to meet his nephew-in-law, Tsar Nicholas II. It was a relaxed family affair. The Tsar, wearing naval uniform, met the King on board the royal yacht *Victoria and Albert*.

In addition to two days of talks there were Royal Family banquets and balls. But back home, there was criticism in the House of Commons, with one MP calling the Tsar 'a common murderer.'

Keir Hardie, the Labour leader, attacked the British government for allowing the visit, claiming the King was condoning atrocities by going to see the Tsar.

In August the King met another of his foreign relatives, Kaiser Wilhelm II of Germany. The government backed the King's desire to meet his nephews to ease the growing tension between the two countries.

Ministers were anxious to learn more about the build-up of German forces, especially the navy. On June 14, the Reichstag had passed a new Navy Bill, which aimed to boost the size of the German fleet. This was happening at a time when spending on British forces had been cut by £2 million in the previous budget.

The Admiralty claimed that the new German dreadnoughts would be the most heavily armed in the world.

CULLINAN DIAMOND CUT

In Amsterdam, the world's biggest diamond, the Cullinan, was cut for King Edward.

The Cullinan was discovered in the Premier Mine in South Africa in 1905 – the largest gem-quality diamond ever discovered. It was sold to the Transvaal government, which presented it to King Edward on his sixty-sixth birthday on November 9, 1907.

The King entrusted the cutting of the stone to the famous Asscher's Diamond Co. in Amsterdam, which had cut the Excelsior and other large gems.

The huge diamond was studied for months and on February 10, 1908, the cutting began. The nine major stones form part of the British Crown Jewels and are in the personal possession of the Royal Family.

The largest stone, the pear-shaped Cullinan I or the 'Star of Africa', weighed 530.20 carats and was placed in the Royal Sceptre. The Cullinan II – a 317.40 carat cushion shaped diamond – was mounted in the Imperial State Crown.

THE CHILD EMPEROR

Emperor Kuang Hsu of China died on November 14 and Child Emperor Pu Yi succeeded to the throne as Hsuan Tung on December 2, at the age of two years ten months.

Overnight, he was treated as a god. Adults, save his wet-nurse, were unable to discipline him and would kneel on the floor in his presence and avoid looking him in the eye.

Pu Yi had been named as heir to the throne by the Empress Dowager Tzu Hsi, who had effectively ruled China since 1861. He was the son of her nephew Prince Chun. The Dowager had disliked her nephew Emperor Kuang Hsu's modernisation programme and, encouraged by powerful allies in the country, had returned to power after she imprisoned him. Tzu Hsi Hsu died shortly after Kuang Hsu, in 1908.

Historical Events

BIRTH OF THE TERRITORIALS

The Territorial Force, which became known as the Territorial Army in 1921, came into existence on April 1. It included the merger of the Yeomanry – a volunteer cavalry corp formed at the time of the French Revolution – along with Army volunteers and nursing reserves.

The force was split into 14 infantry divisions and the same number of cavalry brigades. The training for the new Territorial Army was linked to that of the regular Army, commanded by the General Staff.

EUROPE'S BIGGEST EARTHQUAKE

The biggest earthquake ever recorded in Europe occurred in Sicily on December 28 with over 100,000 people estimated to have died.

Messina, where the great majority lived, was destroyed, killing around half of the inhabitants.

The 7.5-magnitude tremor off the coast of the island was also responsible for deaths on the Italian mainland. The earthquake let loose a massive tidal wave, adding to the chaos.

28th December, 1908, a huge earthquake in Messina killed around 100,000 with search parties working for weeks in the devastated city which was almost totally destroyed. Here, the King and Queen of Italy show their support. British sailors assisted in the search and rescue efforts and were awarded medals for their help.

Social Change

HELPING THE AGED

Prime Minister Herbert Asquith used the budget debate in May to announce his plans for a universal old age pension. The over-seventies were to receive five shillings each, or 7s 6d for a married couple. The only exceptions were those deemed not to have worked to their ability, convicted criminals, the insane and paupers.

The act was passed on June 10, and two months later Chancellor of the Exchequer David Lloyd George travelled to Berlin to study the German system of payment.

The Prime Minister also set about tackling unemployment by increasing local authority grants directed at delayed public utility projects, so that men could be taken on immediately. In an October statement, greeted with cheers in the House of Commons, he also announced that 8,000 seasonal staff would be employed at the Post Office, 2,100 dockyard workers taken on for Board of Admiralty work and a further 24,000 taken into the Special Reserves.

DRINKING HOURS

In an attempt to tackle the problem of drunkenness, the Government introduced a Licensing Bill in February which would cut the number of licensed premises by a third.

On September 27, 500,000 demonstrators marched in Hyde Park after brewing companies laid on trains to ferry them to the capital, and in November 27 the act was thrown out by the House of Lords by a majority of 272 to 96.

Furious at the Lords refusal to pass the bill, cabinet minister Winston Churchill roared, 'We shall send them up a budget in June as shall terrify them. They have started a class war, they had better be careful.'

The social welfare of children was also subject for parliamentary debate in February, when the Children's Bill was published. Aimed at protecting children from abuse, it made it illegal for adults to allow their children to smoke and also set up the groundwork for a fair juvenile justice system.

CHILDREN'S CHAMPION DIES

Reverend Benjamin Waugh, the founder of the National Society for the Prevention of Cruelty to Children, passed away after a long illness on March 11. Having worked tirelessly with the slum children of London since 1866, the Reverend set up the London Society for the Prevention of Cruelty to Children in 1884, changing the name to 'National' five years later. Known as 'the Children's Protector', Waugh and his supporters were instrumental in the passing of the Prevention of Cruelty to Children Act in 1889.

To date, the NSPCC has provided help to over 10 million children.

Fashion

THE REVOLUTION!

French designer Paul Poiret came up with a new style that was to revolutionise female clothing forever. His new day dress and corset mirrored a woman's natural shape, rather than producing the over–exaggerated curves of previous designs, and in this sense it can be seen as the beginning of modern-day fashion.

However, while the bust was freer, the new corsets for straight figures were much longer.

'It was in the name of liberty that I proclaimed the fall of the corset and the adoption of the brassiere which, since then, has won the day,' he stated later. 'Yes, I freed the bust, but I shackled the legs.'

Indeed, the design which came out of the new straight figure was eventually dubbed the 'hobble skirt', as the bottom of the garment was so narrow that women were obliged to take tiny steps.

Poiret's look also spelled the end for the frilly, fussy petticoats, which were replaced with simple silk slips.

Entertainment

FILM

The first newsreel was shown in Paris by the Pathé brothers. The short news clips featured the crowing rooster logo which was to remain familiar to all cinema-goers for decades. Shown before the main feature film, the Pathé newsreel lasted until the late sixties, when it was finally supplanted by television bulletins.

The Pathés achieved another first when their cameraman L. P. Bouvillain recorded a film from an aeroplane.

The Motion Picture Patent Company, also known as 'The Trust', was formed with Thomas Edison as its head. A co-operative of leading film companies, it was designed to protect patents and copyrights but also pushed for standard rates for film prints rented on a weekly basis. The organisation greatly strengthened the US film industry.

Director D.W.Griffiths joined the American Mutoscope and Biograph Company in New York and made his first film, *The Adventures of Dollie*. It was the first of 500 he would make in the next five years.

Also for the Biograph Company, celebrated stage actor Lionel Barrymore made his film debut in *The Paris Hat*. Barrymore would go on to become one of America's favourite screen actors, with roles in *Dr Kildare* and *It's a Wonderful Life*.

Other films released included *Dr Jekyll and Mr Hyde*, *Romeo and Juliet* and *In the Sultan's Power,* the first film totally shot in Los Angeles.

THEATRE

Actor manager Sir John Hare led calls for the creation of a national theatre in honour of William Shakespeare, and a meeting in May was attended by 2,000 people from the worlds of theatre, literature and politics. Lord Lytton chaired the meeting and George Bernard Shaw, H.G.Wells, G.K.Chesterton and Jerome K. Jerome were among those present. A vote in favour of combining the ideas of a national theatre and a memorial to Shakespeare was carried unanimously.

It was also decided the theatre should be built by 1916, the 300th anniversary of the Bard's death.

Elsewhere, a fire at Drury Lane Theatre destroyed the stage but quick thinking by the caretakers, who lowered the fireproof curtain, saved the auditorium. The Playhouse Theatre opened for the first time in January and the Apollo theatre became home to Harry Gabriel Pelissier's *The Follies*, which would run for four years.

Exotic dancer Maud Allan dominated the stage in 1908 with her sensual *Dance of Salome*. Such was her popularity that 90,000 people went to the hitherto unpopular Olympic Games just to see a glimpse of the famous dancer who attended with her friends, the Asquiths (Image courtesy of Russell James, from *The Maud Allan Affair*, published by Remember When).

Fred Karno's travelling troupe *London Comedians* took on a promising young comedian called Charlie Chaplin. His talent was quickly apparent and he soon rose to be star of the show. Two years later, the group travelled to the United States where Chaplin made an instant impression. In 1913, he signed a movie deal and moved to Hollywood.

New drama included Baroness Orczy's *Beau Brocade* and J.M.Synge's *The Tinker's Wedding*.

MUSIC

Columbia Records marketed the first double-sided disc, angering rivals the Victor Company, who had a patent on the technology. Victor sued and, at the court hearing, Columbia's lawyer waved the offending disc in the air and asked, 'If we are to be restricted to one side of the record, which side shall it be?' The patent was overturned and Columbia was able to release the discs.

In classical music, the first symphony of Sir Edward Elgar premiered in Manchester on December 3; *Symphony no.1 in A flat major* was played by the Halle Orchestra, and conducted by Hans Richter. On the first day of the year, Gustav Mahler made his US conducting debut in New York.

BIRTHS

January 10 – Bernard Lee, British actor and James Bond's 'M'.
January 16 – Ethel Merman, US actress.
February 22 – John Mills, British actor.
March 5 – Rex Harrison, British actor.
March 20 – Michael Redgrave, British actor.
May 20 – James Stewart, US actor.
May 30 – Mel Blanc, US voice actor.
June 10 – Robert Cummings, US actor.
October 6 – Carole Lombard, US actress.
December 18 – Celia Johnson, British actress.

Literature

UNCLE REMUS MOVES ON

Joel Chandler Harris, author of the 'Uncle Remus' stories, died in July from cirrhosis of the liver. Born in Georgia to a poor seamstress, who was deserted by Harris's father soon after his birth, Harris began work at 16 for a local plantation owner. Here he learned to write by setting newspaper type for his employer's trade newspaper, printed on the premises.

Crucially, the young Harris also befriended the plantation slaves, known as Uncle George Terrell, Old Harbett and Aunt Crissy. They were to become the models for Uncle Remus, Aunt Tempy and other characters in his books.

A published author and respected journalist by the age of 20, Harris introduced the fictional Uncle Remus in a newspaper's editorials, relating the stories he would tell when he popped into the office. Brer Rabbit, Brer Fox and the Tar Baby were among the characters in the collection, which was soon large enough for a book. In 1880, *Uncle Remus: His Songs and His Sayings—The Folklore of the Old Plantation* was published and sold 10,000 copies in four months. In all, Harris wrote 185 tales.

TOAD OF TOAD HALL

A children's novel written by a secretary for the Bank of England, Kenneth Grahame, was published. *The Wind in the Willows* was a charming tale of a friendship between four woodland animals, Rat, Mole, Badger and the grand but silly Toad of Toad Hall. Although it sold reasonably, the book was given a tremendous boost by Winnie the Pooh creator A.A.Milne, who adapted it for the stage as *Toad of Toad Hall*.

Eventually, the book made Grahame enough money to leave his detested position at the bank and retire to the country where, like his characters, he spent much of his time 'messing about in boats.'

Other books published this year included Beatrix Potter's *The Tale of Jemima Puddle-Duck*, Lucy Maud Montgomery's *Anne of Green Gables* and E.M. Forster's *Room with a View*.

Beatrix Potter's Jemima Puddleduck was hatched in 1908 and has proved a perennial favourite ever since. This image is taken from the plate by Royal Albert, one of many collectables featuring the adorable duck.

Actress Sarah Berhardt also published her autobiography *My Double Life*.

BIRTHS

January 9 – Simone de Beauvoir, French philosopher.
May 28 – Ian Fleming, British author and James Bond creator.
August 21 – M. M. Kaye, British author of *Far Pavilions*.

DEATHS

July 3 – Joel Chandler Harris, US author.

Architecture

LONDON EXPOSITION

In order to celebrate the new Entente Cordiale between the two countries, a Franco-British Exhibition was held in London. A 200 acre plot of agricultural land in Shepherd's Bush was set aside for the event, and many new buildings erected to house the collections of art, furniture and industrial displays from France and Britain.

The largest of the buildings, the Court of Honour, was surrounded by an artificial lake measuring 400 feet by 100 feet and, straddled by an ornamental bridge.

However, event co-ordinator Imre Kiralfy attracted criticism from the architects involved after presenting them with steel frameworks of his own design to work on, leaving them minimal scope for creativity. Critics also complained that the buildings did not sit well together, with the French opting for an art nouveau approach and the British leaning towards classic lines.

The centrepiece, the Court of Honour, also came in for some criticism for its Oriental style. The eminent art critic Sir Walter Armstrong wrote, 'It is neither French nor English, but Mohamedan-Hindoo, and the other buildings have more in common with the architecture of Spanish-America or the Baroque of a united Germany than with anything in the two countries involved.'

A complete reproduction of an Irish village, Bally Maclinton, was a popular attraction. It included an exact replica of 'MacKinley Cottage' – where the ancestor of the late American president was born.

Bridge in Court of Honour, Franco-British Exhibition, London, 1908

The White City of the Franco-British Exhibition would leave its mark on London and was on the exact site where the BBC stands (for now). Eight million people attended the event which spanned 140 acres.

The recreation of the Irish village was one of the highlights of the Franco-British Exhibition. There were 150 'coleens' (Irish girls) who exhibited household labour. There was also an art gallery and manufacturing displays in the village, which was called Ballymaclinton.

On the Western Lagoon.
Franco-British Exhibition, London, 1908.

VALENTINE'S SERIES.
COPYRIGHT.

One of many postcards produced for the seven-month exhibition which celebrated the Entente Cordiale of 1904 and is the first of the Exposition's organised by two countries.

The Olympic Games was staged within the exhibition at a specially built stadium which had a pool and a 400m cycle and running track. A flip-flap (see pxx) enabled visitors to have a panoramic view of the area. The stadium was built in only two years.

The white buildings in the exhibition area gave name to the area's name, White City, both during and after the event. The elegant architecture was complemented by the universal colour scheme. The main entrance was on Uxbridge Road.

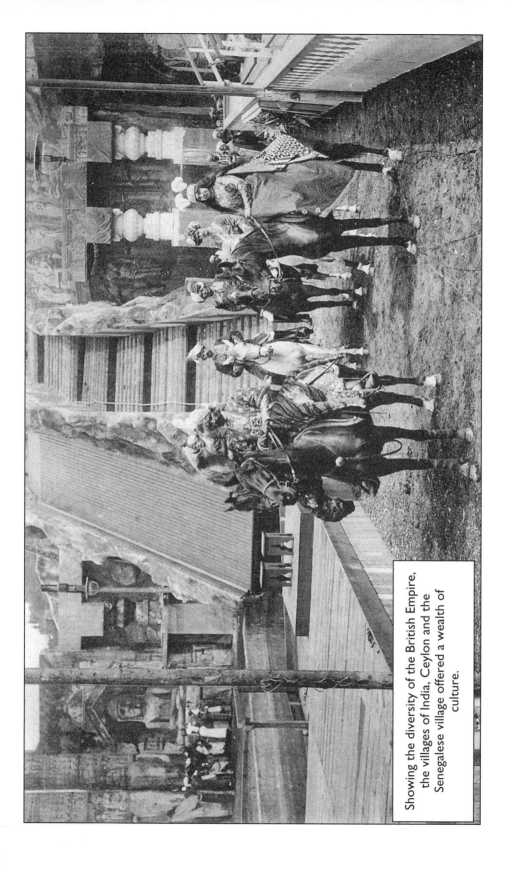

Showing the diversity of the British Empire, the villages of India, Ceylon and the Senegalese village offered a wealth of culture.

The universally white buildings led to the West London area being renamed White City.

A huge stadium and a swimming pool were also built for the summer's Olympic Games.

NEW YORK'S TALLEST

The Singer building in Manhattan became the tallest in the world when it was completed in 1908. Designed by Ernest Flagg, the 12-storey, steel framed structure stood at 187 metres (612 feet). Built in the baroque style from red brick and limestone, as the headquarters of the sewing machine manufacturers, it was surpassed a year later by the Metropolitan Life Insurance Company Tower on Madison Avenue. The Singer building was demolished in 1968.

UNITY TEMPLE

Frank Lloyd Wright's revolutionary temple was completed in Oak Park, Illinois. The great architect stated that his intention was to 'not merely create a religious structure, but one that fitly embodies the principles of liberal religion for which this church stands . . . unity, truth, beauty, simplicity, freedom and reason'.

The Unitarian Universalist church was influenced by the Cubist movement and constructed from concrete squares. In order to accommodate services at the same time as community events, Wright divided the temple and the event space with a low, middle gallery, and put in place two outer doors that could be approached from opposite sides.

Art

DUBLIN LEADS THE WAY

The world's first public gallery devoted entirely to Modern Art was founded in Dublin's Harcourt Street by Hugh Lane. A Cornish art restorer turned dealer, Lane had a great affection for Ireland having spent many years visiting his aunt, Lady Gregory, in County Galway. On one such visit he came across the works of Nathaniel Hone and John Butler Yeats and became a passionate advocate for a gallery in Dublin, where the public could have access to national and international art.

After a successful exhibition in London, Lane persuaded contemporary Irish artists to donate works to his collection – as well as buying many paintings himself, including *La Musique aux Tuileries* by Manet, *Sur la Plage* by Degas, *Les Parapluies* by Renoir and *La Cheminée* by Vuillard. The Municipal Gallery of Modern Art was originally set up in temporary premises. Tragically, Lane was killed in 1915, on board HMS *Lusitania* when it was sunk by a German submarine, and never saw his gallery permanently housed.

RUBBISH ART

A group of artists whose work depicted the urban reality of grubby streets and city life had become known as the 'Ash Can School'. Begun by Robert Henri some years before, the group focussed on everyday lives and ordinary people, painting in a loose style with a dark palette.

In 1908 a group known as 'The Eight', the leading lights in the movement, held their first exhibition at New York's Macbeth Gallery. It was a statement against Modern Art in America, because it was selected and organised by the artists themselves, and offered no judgement or prizes.

MONET BURNS THE MONEY

In a fit of depression in Paris, Claude Monet destroyed 15 of his major water garden paintings just days before they were to be exhibited at the Durand-Ruel gallery in Paris. Ever critical of his own work, Monet was notorious for such flamboyant destruction and was convinced the works, valued at around £20,000, were unsatisfactory.

Travel and Transport

A FARE FIGHT FOR ATLANTIC CROSSING

The price of travel across the Atlantic fell sharply at the start of the year as the two main shipping lines, White Star and Cunard, battled it out to attract more passengers. Both lines had recently cut their fares twice so that second-class tickets fell by as much as 45 shillings and third-class by 30 shillings. But by February, the two rivals agreed to end the price-cutting war and fares nearly doubled.

Later in the year, Cunard's two mighty passenger ships set Atlantic crossing speed records. The *Mauretania* crossed eastbound from the US in five days, five minutes. And the *Lusitania* westbound from Britain in four days, 20 hours and 12 minutes.

BATTLE FOR THE SKIES

Henri Farman, 'the Flying Frenchman', won the coveted 50,000 francs prize for the first heavier-than-air aircraft to cover a circuit of at least one kilometre.

He took off from a large field in Issy-les-Moulineaux, five miles south of Paris, on January 13, in a biplane weighing 300 lbs powered by a 50 hp engine. In front of officials of the Aero Club of France, he flew around a pylon 500 metres away and returned.

Farman flew at 24 miles an hour, at a height of around 25 feet, and the whole flight took just one minute 28 seconds. It was heralded as proof that the new aircraft would in future replace steerable balloons in air travel.

In March, Farman succeeded in making the first aeroplane flight with a passenger. Both the French Army and US Army took a keen interest in this increasingly reliable form of transport.

On September 17, Lieutenant Thomas E. Selfridge of the US Army, died in an aircraft piloted by Orville Wright, who was seriously injured. The tragedy occurred as Wright flew his biplane on army trials at Fort Myer, Virginia.

In front of 2,000 spectators, the aircraft slowly climbed but, as it turned,

Henri Farman, 'The Flying Frenchman' landing to win the Grand Prix.

a blade on the left propeller broke causing the plane to fall from a height of 75 feet. The lieutenant suffered a fractured skull and never regained consciousness. Wright had a broken left leg and four broken ribs

Orville Wright had been conducting a series of flight trials in front of senior army officers to demonstrate that the aircraft met all the requirements set by the War Department. The US Secretary of War, Luke Wright, said that the accident would not stop the trials.

Meanwhile, Orville's brother Wilbur topped a series of record-breaking flights in France by staying aloft for more than an hour with a passenger. He won himself a $100,000 patents deal with a French company who had already ordered 50 of his aircraft. Orville recovered from his injuries and he too made several successful passenger flights that autumn.

MODEL T DRIVES IN

Driving for the masses was set on course when Henry Ford's new Model T rolled off his assembly line in Detroit. It replaced the existing Model A, made for the past five years, and fulfilled Ford's promise, made the previous year to produce 'a motor car for the great multitude'.

His aim was to provide a car cheap enough for anyone on a good salary to buy, yet still use quality components based on 'the simplest designs that modern engineering can devise'. His revolutionary assembly line enabled him to produce these cars cheaply in mass volume.

The new model, produced only in black, was nicknamed the 'Tin Lizzy' and sold for around $900.

Toys

CHILTERN BEARS

The Chiltern Toy Works was founded in Buckinghamshire in 1908 by Josef Eisenmann and his son-in-law Leon Rees.

Josef and his brother Gabriel had started Chiltern Toys as a toy export company in the late Nineteenth Century. Gabriel was based in Germany and Josef in London.

The fledgling Chiltern Toy Works initially produced dolls, but the popularity of teddy bears continued to increase and the company made its first bear in 1915. Soon it became a well-known teddy bear manufacturer.

Sport

LONDON OLYMPICS

After just two years preparation, the London Olympics took place with great aplomb. The centrepiece was the White City Stadium, alongside the Franco-British Exhibition, where the athletic events took place.

A total of 2,035 athletes, representing 21 countries, took part in the Games which, for the first time, included the winter sport of ice-skating.

The most famous incident that occurred was in the Marathon. Italian runner Dorando Pietri was the first to enter the stadium, well ahead of the pack, but he was close to exhaustion. Bewildered, he ran the wrong way around the track, corrected himself and fell to the ground five times before well-meaning stewards helped him across the line.

This meant he was disqualified and the medal went to American Johnny Hayes who was second over the line. But such was the feeling of public warmth towards Pietri that he was presented with a gold cup by Queen Alexandra in recognition of his efforts.

The distance from the start of the Marathon to the finish at the stadium was established at this Games as 26 miles 385 yards. This unusual distance

The 1908 Olympic Games took place in London at the new White City Stadium as part of the Franco-British Exhibition. Visitors included the royal family, the Asquiths and the notorious Maud Allan. The flip-flap enabled visitors to the exhibition to see over the whole area, including the stadium.

was so that the course would cover the ground from Windsor Castle to White City Stadium, where the Royal Family would have a perfect view of the finishing line.

For the first time, judges came from various countries, rather that just the host nation. But it was the host nation that dominated the Games with Britain winning 56 gold medals, the US in second place with 23 and Sweden third with eight.

W.G. GRACE RETIRES FROM FIRST-CLASS CRICKET

Cricketing legend W.G. Grace retired from first-class cricket at the age of 59 when he took the field for the Gentlemen of England against Surrey in the first game of the season on August 31.

Although he later played other games, this was his last at this level in nearly a century of cricket during which he became one of the most famous players of all time.

In county cricket, he played for Gloucestershire and the London County Cricket Club and made his test debut in 1880. Two years later he made England's first ever century and captained the national team from 1888 to 1899.

His artistry with the bat and his spin bowling delighted the crowds. He set numerous cricketing records but it was also his startling look – bulky and rather scruffy with a long black beard – that made him such a loved and recognisable figure. Dr Grace did much to increase the popularity of the game.

Famous for his gamesmanship and arrogance, he was known to shout 'Miss it' when fielders attempted to catch him out and often argued with umpires. One of the many stories about him was when he was given 'out' early in a county match. He refused to go, declaring, 'They've come to see me bat, not you umpire. Play on!'

FIRST BLACK HEAVYWEIGHT BOXING CHAMP

Texan boxer Jack Johnson became the first black man to hold the world heavyweight champion's title when he defeated Tommy Burns in Sydney, Australia, on December 26.

Born in Galveston on March 31, 1878, Johnson started boxing as a sparring partner and turned professional in 1897.

By 1902, he had won at least 50 fights and won his first title on February 3, 1903, beating 'Denver' Ed Martin over 20 rounds for the World Coloured Heavyweight Championship.

His efforts to win the full title were thwarted as World Heavyweight Champion Jim Jeffries refused to face him because he was black. Johnson was, however, able to fight former champion Bob Fitzsimmons in July 1907, and knocked him out in two rounds.

He eventually got his chance for the big prize when he faced up to Canadian Burns in Sydney. The event attracted huge attention, with around 20,000 spectators packed into the stadium.

Police stopped the fight in the 14th round after Burns had been knocked out for eight seconds. They moved in as he groggily got to his feet but was unable to defend himself from a further torrent of blows.

A towering man, Johnson was an early example of the celebrity athlete, endorsing various products, appearing regularly in the press and later on radio and in motion pictures. He faced and defeated a string of 'Great White Hopes' and enjoyed his success and wealth to the full – wearing expensive suits and jewellery and boasting of his accomplishments. He was to hold the world title until 1915.

The Home

IDEAL HOMES

The *Daily Mail* 'Ideal Home Exhibition' opened at London's Olympia for the first time. Packed with labour-saving devices for the well-to-do householder, the exhibition was split into 12 distinct sections, including food and cookery, furniture and decoration. New gadgets such as electric fires and kettles, gas cookers and washing machines were on show as well as the latest model of vacuum cleaner, now small enough to be used in houses.

Not only did the show appeal to fashionable society ladies, who could view the latest trends in furniture, but with domestic servants becoming less and less affordable, the new breed of housewife could find some help for her daily chores.

The brainchild of Wareham Smith, advertising manager of the *Daily Mail,* the show was intended to raise revenue and awareness of the paper by attracting middle-class women with disposable income. But royalty and visiting celebrities were to be frequent guests in the coming years.

Throughout its 100-year history, the exhibition has since been responsible for introducing a myriad of appliances, including the microwave and the electric fridge.

The Changing Role of Women

PROVIDING PROOF

In answer to the doubts of leading politicians Balfour and Asquith, as to whether women really wanted the vote, Christabel Pankhurst set about organising a series of mass demonstrations to prove the cause had widespread support.

On February 11, just after the Queen's Speech – which had no mention of votes for women – the 'Women's Parliament' met at Caxton Hall in London and marched on the House of Commons. They also hired two vans which were driven to Parliament Square loaded with suffragettes, who burst out and stormed the Commons. Fifty-four women were arrested and the majority were sentenced to two months in jail.

In March, a demonstration at the Albert Hall was attended by 7,000, and on June 21 a rally in Hyde Park attracted some 200,000 supporters, both male and female. Christabel Pankhurst, who was the main speaker, was convinced that this would finally show the Government that the cause had widespread support. However, April had seen the inauguration of Herbert Asquith, who was a fierce opponent of women's votes, as the new Prime Minister.

The summer months also saw the WSPU instigate a campaign of stone throwing at Government buildings, and on June 30 a large group marched on Downing Street to break the windows of the Prime Minister's house. Twenty-seven were arrested and jailed in Holloway prison.

The demonstrations of 1908 also led to the adoption of a 'uniform' for the first time. Mrs Pethick-Lawrence asked marchers to wear purple, white and green. Later she explained that white symbolised 'purity in public as well as private life', green stood for the hope of a 'new spring tide' and purple stood for dignity.

PRISON FOR MRS P.

The Women's Social and Political Union (WPSU) stepped up their militant campaign and Emmeline Pankhurst found herself in prison twice this year.

During her first six-week sentence, on charges of obstructing the police within the proscribed area of Parliament, she wrote of the conditions in Holloway jail. Revealing the meagre rations and stark surroundings, she referred to her cellmates as 'all so sad and weak and feeble'.

'All the hours seem very long in prison,' she wrote. 'The sun can never get in . . . and every day so changeless and uninteresting. One grows almost too tired to go through to the exercise yard and yet one has a yearning for the open air.'

The Government relented in March and released Mrs Pankhurst in time for the Albert Hall Rally on the 19th. She walked onto stage to huge applause from thousands of supporters.

In October, she was in court again, alongside daughter Christabel, following a rowdy demonstration in which she had handed out leaflets encouraging supporters to 'rush' the House of Commons. Two cabinet members – David Lloyd George and Henry Gladstone – were among the witnesses called to the stand, where one lady attested that she had been more jostled at society weddings than she had on the night in question.

A rousing speech was met with cheers and tears by Mrs Pankhurst's female supporters. 'We are not here because we are law-breakers,' she told the courtroom. 'We are here in our effort to become law-makers.'

The judge was unmoved by her plea, however, and the two women were sentenced to three months for conduct likely to cause a breach of the peace.

LADY MAYORESS

Trailblazing doctor Elizabeth Garrett Anderson became the first female to be elected mayor in Britain, at the age of 72. The daughter of a self-made businessman, Elizabeth was already a leading light in the advancement of women, having been the first female to become a doctor in 1865. Refused entry to medical college, she became a nurse and attended lectures given to trainee doctors at the hospital. Discovering that the rules of the governing body, the Society of Apothecaries, did not specifically ban women, she insisted on taking the exam and was granted the necessary certificate to practice. Soon afterwards, the society changed the regulations to bar women.

With the help of her father, Elizabeth started her own practice in London and a year later set up a dispensary for women.

Science

GEIGER COUNTER INVENTED

German physicist Hans Geiger, together with Ernest Rutherford, professor of physics at the University of Manchester, developed a device to detect radiation, which later became known as the 'Geiger Counter'.

This counter was only capable of detecting alpha particles but in 1928 Geiger and Walther Müller, one of Geiger's PhD students, improved the instrument so that it could detect all kinds of ionizing radiation.

A CLEAR WINNER

Cellophane was invented by Swiss textile engineer Jacques E. Brandenberger, who first thought of the idea for a clear, protective, packaging layer in 1900.

Brandenberger was seated at a restaurant when a customer spilt wine onto the tablecloth. As the waiter replaced the cloth, Brandenberger decided that he would invent a clear coating that could be applied to cloth, making it waterproof.

His experiments led to a liquid viscose but when it was applied to cloth it made the material too stiff. However, it peeled off in a transparent film which led to new and better uses.

He developed the first machine for the manufacture of transparent sheets of regenerated cellulose, producing Cellophane. Its low permeability to air, grease and bacteria made it ideal for food packaging.

WASHING MACHINE

The electric washing machine was first mass-produced in 1908 by the Hurley Machine Company of Chicago. It was called 'Mighty Thor' and was invented by Alva J. Fisher.

Chapter Ten

1909

Politics

GERMANY BUILDS MORE WARSHIPS

GERMAN NAVAL expansion continued to worry Britain. The First Lord of the Admiralty, Reginald McKenna, told the Government that Germany was likely to have 13 new dreadnoughts completed by 1911 alone, on top of those already in service. Plans were laid for six new British dreadnoughts, along with new cruisers and armoured destroyers.

'PEOPLE'S BUDGET' FLAMES CLASS WAR

David Lloyd George, Chancellor of the Exchequer, introduced the most radical Budget in the nation's history on April 29.

It proposed a large rise in taxes to pay for rearmament and a programme of social reform – including the new Old Age Pensions Act.

In introducing what he called the 'People's Budget' Lloyd George argued that social reform could not be postponed until rearmament was completed.

Standard rate of tax on earned income would stay at 9d in the pound up to £2,000 and 1 shilling and 2d above that level. But a new 'supertax' of 6d in the pound would be levied on the 10,000 people with incomes over £5,000 a year.

Other measures included an increase in death duties on the estates of the wealthy and higher taxation on cars, alcohol, tobacco and petrol. The Budget also introduced labour exchanges and a children's allowance on income tax.

It was instantly condemned by the Tory opposition as attacking the propertied classes on whom the prosperity and stability of the country depended. They warned that the new death duties could lead to economies on large estates – to the detriment of tradesmen and the working classes.

Winston Churchill warned the Lords that there would be a fight to the finish if they vetoed the Budget. When it was ultimately rejected, the Prime Minister, Herbert Asquith, subsequently moved a motion to dissolve Parliament, declaring the act to be a breach of the constitution.

Lloyd George toured the country, addressing working-class crowds, declaring that the rich landowners who filled the red benches of the Lords would rather see the food of the masses taxed rather than pay for important measures to fight poverty from their own overflowing pockets.

The Liberals were returned to Parliament and the Lords were finally forced to accept the Budget on April 28, 1910.

BIRTHS

Jan 22 – Sithu U Thant, Burmese statesman and Secretary General of the United Nations.
July 18 – Andrei Gromyko, Soviet statesman.

Royalty

CHEERS AND JEERS FOR THE KING

King Edward VII visited Berlin where he was met by cheering crowds.

King Edward VII played the diplomat once more as he met up with the same two foreign royal relations as he had the previous year. In February, he and Queen Alexandra arrived in Berlin on an official visit where the King and Kaiser Wilhelm reaffirmed their friendship and pledged to work for lasting good relations between their countries.

The King, wearing German military uniform, rode with the Kaiser in an open-top carriage through the streets to cheering crowds.

But he received some criticism in August when Tsar Nicholas II arrived in Britain. The Tsar was honoured with much pomp and ceremony, including a formal review of the Royal Navy. But many workers staged demonstrations in protest at the visit of the Tsar, who ruthlessly suppressed human rights and political and social reform in his country.

The new Turkish Sultan, Mehmet V promised 'liberty, equality and justice' for his new subjects after the violence and corruption of his brother's reign.

After a revolution, 12-year-old Ahmed Mirza replaced his father as the Shah of Persia. The country was renamed Iran in 1935.

CROWNS TOPPLED

Two imperial heads of state were overthrown this year for their despotic behaviour. In Constantinople there were celebrations in April after the tyrannical Sultan Abdul Hamid II was forced to abdicate.

The Sultan had suspended Parliament in 1878 but the revolution in 1908 by the nationalist Young Turks had pressurised him into restoring it. And it was this Parliament that voted unanimously to depose him.

The statement announcing his replacement by his brother, Mehmet V, accused him of committing massacres, breaking the law and squandering the wealth of the Ottoman Empire.

The Sultan was arrested in his exotic palace and Mehmet took the throne, promising 'liberty, equality and justice' for all his subjects.

The Persian Shah, Mohammad Ali Mirza, was also deposed after he accepted the principle of constitution but then annulled the new law providing for elections and postponed the constitution indefinitely. The Shah was finally toppled after a turbulent two years on the throne by a revolution of the Nationalist Party.

He was succeeded by his 12-year old son, Ahmed Mirza, following four days of fighting in Tehran.

BIRTHS

April 30 – Queen Juliana of the Netherlands.

DEATHS

December 17 – King Leopold II of Belgium.

Historical Events

PRINCE ITO ASSASSINATED

Japan's most senior statesman, Prince Ito, was assassinated on October 26 by a Korean nationalist.

Ito had recently retired as Governor-General of Korea, where he had made many enemies for his harsh suppression of anyone who opposed Japanese rule. He was shot dead in Manchuria at the age of 68.

The former Prime Minister of Japan had a leading role in the framing of his country's constitution and in building Japan into a world power.

He had studied in Europe and saw the necessity for political change in Japan in order for it to join the ranks of modern civilised countries.

During the war with Russia, he had been at the head of the body of elder statesmen who acted in an advisory capacity to the Emperor. At the close of the war, and after Japan took charge in Korea, Marquis Ito, as he was then, was raised to the rank of Prince by the Emperor and sent to Korea as Governor-General.

PROHIBITION MOVEMENT GAINS GROUND

Alcohol was becoming increasingly hard to find in the US as the prohibition movement continued its anti-drinking campaign. Whilst some states outlawed all alcoholic sales, others let local towns decide. In New York state, for example, 315 towns had banned saloons by the beginning of the year. And in Ohio, saloons were closed in 57 of the state's 66 counties.

POLE TO POLE

On January 9, a British expedition led by Lieutenant Edward Shackleton reached a point closer to the South Pole than any other explorers before him.

Weak from lack of food, the explorers planted the Union Jack, stayed a few minutes and then turned round and headed for home.

But at the other end of the world, there was a big controversy between two American explorers.

After five previous attempts, Commander Robert E. Peary of the US

IN SIGHT OF THE SOUTH POLE.

LIEUT. SHACKLETON'S GREAT FEAT.

111 MILES FROM THE GOAL.

MAGNETIC POLE REACHED.

THE QUEEN'S FLAG HOISTED.

GREAT SCIENTIFIC DISCOVERIES.

EXCLUSIVE CABLE BY LIEUT. SHACKLETON.

The long and historic cablegram which Lieutenant Shackleton sends to us from Half-Moon Bay, New Zealand, tells the wonderful story of his momentous Antarctic expedition. The achievements which he records are by far the greatest in Polar history. He has approached nearer than any other discoverer, living or dead, has ever drawn to either Pole.

On January 9, 1909, he hoisted the Union Jack, given to him by her Majesty the Queen, at a point 88deg. 23min. of south latitude and 162deg. of east longitude, distant only 111 ... from ... th Pol...

Shackleton's adventures were recorded in *The Daily Mail.*

Lt Edward Shackleton explored closer to the South Pole than anyone else, returning to great acclaim on the Nimrod which was met with cheering crowds.

Navy arrived at the North Pole on April 6. But when Peary returned home he discovered that a rival explorer, Brooklyn doctor Frederick A. Cook, had claimed that he had reached the Pole a year earlier.

Cook had accompanied Peary on one of his previous expeditions to the Pole. Peary dismissed Cook's claim and said that he interviewed two Eskimos in the doctor's party who said that Cook turned back a long way from the Pole.

Although there was also some scepticism over Peary's claim, the National Geographic Society accepted it and presented him with a gold medal. By December, Cook was disgraced when his Eskimo companions testified that he had not come within 20 miles of the Pole. Furthermore, his claim to be the first man to climb Mount McKinley – the highest mountain in the USA – was proved false by one of the mountain guides.

A committee appointed by the University of Copenhagen found that documents provided by Cook 'do not contain certain observations and information which can be regarded as proof that Dr Cook reached the North Pole'. Some hinted that Cook had forged them.

Social Change

THE ELDERLY REJOICE

As the New Year dawned, 400,000 people over the age of 70 were entitled to pick up their first Old Age Pension, and post offices around the country were inundated.

Many were overjoyed at the five shilling payments, which meant that relying on charity was no longer necessary. Newspapers reported that the people queuing at post offices were patient and polite and had dressed up in their smartest clothes for the occasion.

In the 1939 book *Lark Rise*, Flora Thompson described the scenes at the post offices around the country:

> *At first when they went to the Post Office to draw it, tears of gratitude would run down the cheeks of some, and they would say as they picked up their money, 'God bless that Lloyd George . . . and God bless you, miss!'*

However, it was not such a happy new year for one new pensioner in Bishop Stortford, Essex, where he picked up his first five shillings and promptly dropped dead.

The popularity of the pension took even David Lloyd George by surprise and, in March, he announced that it had proved more expensive than he had expected. In April's Budget he was forced to raise taxes to cover the cost.

LAND OF LITTLE HOPE AND GLORY

A report by the Royal Commission on the Poor Laws, published in February, slammed the treatment of the poor in Britain and claimed that Elgar's *Land of Hope and Glory* was 'a mockery and a falsehood'.

The commission sat for three years, had 200 meetings and visited numerous boards and institutions around the UK, interviewing over 1,300 witnesses. They found that 928,671 people had classed themselves as paupers and were receiving public aid; 'In other words, one in every 44 persons in England and Wales was a pauper on January 1, 1908.'

Conditions in which many were forced to live were 'a discredit and a peril to the whole community' and a study of the nation's workhouses revealed some shocking results.

The committee members visited 350 workhouses and found appalling conditions, with up to 100 men crammed into two rooms, 40 women and children sharing a dormitory and children as young as 18 months working in the kitchen. Of the 8,483 babies born in 1907, 4,050 had died within a year.

The report concluded that children should no longer be put in workhouses and that the powers for child placement should be removed from the Boards of Guardians and placed with the local authorities.

Other suggestions included aid for the 'unemployed of good character', the formation of a unified state health service and tighter employment laws for boys under 15.

The committee were unanimous in their conclusion that the current system needed to be dramatically overhauled but did not always agree on the solutions. Fabian Society luminary Mrs Beatrice Webb and three others produced a second document, or minority report, which called for a Ministry of Labour to tackle unemployment and for public money to be spent on necessary work such as coastal defences.

In a debate in the House of Commons in June, it was agreed by all sides that it was unacceptable to place children in workhouses. The president of the Local Government Board, John Burns, vowed to ensure that all sick children would be moved out of workhouses as soon as possible. He also revealed that 1,000 sick children had already been moved to an institution on the 'healthy breezy downs of Surrey'.

In August, thousands of slum children were treated to a fortnight's free holiday in the country.

The problem of homelessness was on the increase, especially in London. In November, the Salvation Army reported that it was feeding up to 640 vagrants on the Embankment every evening.

Fashion

AMERICAN EXPERIENCE

Chicago businessman Gordon Selfridge opened his flagship store in London's Oxford Street on March 15, with the slogan 'All your shopping under one roof'. The first store was purpose-built and Selfridges offered six acres of floor space. Selfridges encouraged people to spend the whole day inside, with such features as a reading room, a lounge and a roof garden as well as a restaurant. The displays were open and the goods easy to inspect, which was a huge innovation in stylish shopping. The layout was also designed to take the snobbery and class divide out of the world of fashion.

The top-quality goods were reasonably priced but for those with less cash, there was the UK's first bargain basement.

The opening was heralded by an advertising campaign of un-precedented magnitude, including 104 full-page adverts in 18 national newspapers, and the first five days saw a million people pass through the doors.

While the Americans were making a splash in the UK, British fashion designer Lucile had her eye on the Big Apple. Lady Duff-Gordon spent Christmas with her friend Elsie de Wolfe in New York and was surprised by the lack of style she found there. She noted that smart ladies were wearing copies of the latest hats from Paris but 'had chosen them indiscriminately and without taste'. It was time, she concluded, to show New Yorkers a thing or two about fashion.

Within six weeks, a Lucile house opened in West Thirty-Sixth Street and became 'the first English swell to trade in New York', charging $500 for a personal consultation.

SWEATED LABOUR EXPOSED

After years of visiting factories, workshops and homeworkers in the rag trade, Adele Meyer and Clementina Black published *Makers of our Clothes*. Their findings highlighted the appalling pay and conditions that were behind the boom in ready-made clothing and even, in some cases, the higher priced bespoke market.

Many of the seamstresses worked in cramped conditions, with perhaps 50 sewing machines to a room, for 11 hours a day, earning as little as 4s 6d a week. A factory worker might earn around £1 a week and home workers, who often had to buy their own thread and pay for the rental of machines, were paid by the garment. One case study showed that the seamstress was paid 12s for a 'seven seamed skirt, 45 inches long, which had four rows of stitching at each seam and 12 rows at the foot.'

The authors concluded that for the vast majority of workers 'life is a steady round of work at high pressure combined with a ceaseless effort to make a weekly ten shillings equal to a pound'.

The clothing industry was by no means alone in providing cheaper goods through sweated labour, but the huge demand for high fashion at reasonable prices meant that thousands of women, who received lower pay than men, were working long hours for very little.

THE ULTIMATE FASHION MAGAZINE

In New York, a struggling fashion journal called *Vogue* was the latest purchase for publisher Condé Nast. With the help of Edna Woolman Chase, who had worked her way up from the magazine's mail room to the unofficial position of assistant editor, he set about reshaping it into a style bible for upmarket women.

In 1911, Chase became editor and by 1920, according to *The Man Who Was Vogue* by Caroline Seebohm, the profits had risen from $5,000 to $400,000.

Entertainment

FILM

Vaudeville actor Roscoe 'Fatty' Arbuckle joined the Selig Polyscope Company in July and made his film debut in the short comedy *Ben's Kid*. The overweight actor was surprisingly agile and his brand of slapstick comedy a huge hit. He continued to make films for Selig until 1913, when he became the star of Mack Sennett's *Keystone Cops* series. By 1919, 'Fatty' Arbuckle was a megastar and was the first actor to sign a $1 million deal. Two years later, tragedy struck when he was accused of raping and murdering an aspiring actress at a party.

The three resulting trials were huge media events and, although

Arbuckle was acquitted in 1922, with an apology from the jury, the mud stuck and his career was in tatters. It was ten years before he was to act again, with a series of short comedies for Warner Brothers. After their completion, in 1933, the studio signed him for a feature film and Fatty was said to be over the moon. The same night, at the age of 46, he had a heart attack and died.

While holding auditions for the film *Pippa Passes* in April, D.W.Griffiths came across an ambitious young actress called Mary Pickford. Just turned 17, Mary had previously toured the United States in shows with her family and had appeared in a Broadway play with the then unknown Cecil B. DeMille. Griffiths felt she wasn't right for the film but was so taken with her innocent charm that he signed her up to the Biograph Company at $10 dollars a day, twice the amount other actors were receiving.

Miss Pickford certainly proved to be worth the investment. That year alone she appeared in over 50 movies and within five years she was one of America's biggest stars and had earned the nickname 'The World's Sweetheart'. She would go on to become a co-founder of United Artists with Griffiths, Charlie Chaplin and her soon-to-be husband Douglas Fairbanks in 1919.

Also making his film debut this year was Japan's Matsunosuke Onoe, who would star in over 1,000 films and become the first superstar of Japanese cinema.

In the UK, Parliament passed the first legislation which sought to regulate the film industry. The Cinematograph Act laid down fire and safety regulations and required all cinemas to be issued with a licence by the local authority. However, after a court case in which the London County Council prosecuted a cinema owner for opening on a Sunday, the powers of local authorities began to stretch way beyond the fire regulations, with some even interfering with the content of film. The act had given a legal basis for censorship and laid the foundations for the British Board of Film Censors, formed in 1912.

THEATRE

In theatre, a row over censorship had already boiled over into the House of Commons. A select committee was set up to investigate the powers of the Lord Chamberlain, who had the sole right to censor and ban new plays. The event proved a huge public spectacle as famous authors and playwrights flocked to Westminster to testify. Henry James, John Galsworthy, Thomas Hardy and H.G.Wells were among the notaries present and George Bernard Shaw made an impassioned speech in which he declared: 'The censor has my livelihood and my good name absolutely at his disposal, without any law to administer – a control past the last pitch of despotism.'

As many of his plays, including *Mrs Warren's Profession,* had fallen victim to the Lord Chamberlain's axe, Shaw was a passionate opponent of dramatic censorship and campaigned against it until the end of his life. In August 1909, despite the censor's ban, his latest play *The Sewing Up of Blanco Posnet* was performed in Dublin.

Despite the best efforts of the literary giants, the Lord Chamberlain retained his powers for a further 58 years.

Performing for the first time in Paris, in May, the 'Ballets Russes' took the city by storm. Presented by Serge Diaghilev, the troop performed the two ballets *Prince Igor* and *Les Sylphides* with Vaslav Nijinsky and Anna Pavlova in the lead roles. Critics were charmed by Pavlova and bowled over by the technical perfection of Nijinsky, with one describing him as 'the power of youth, drunk with rhythm, terrifying in his muscular energy'.

MUSIC

The career of Enrico Caruso was threatened for the second time by polyps on the larynx. In April, he sailed from New York to Italy where he was admitted to a private hospital in Milan. The operation was successful but the recurring problem was to plague him for the remainder of his career.

In classical music, this year saw the first performances of Maurice Ravel's *Gaspard de la Nuit* in Paris and Rachmaninoff's *Piano Concerto Number 3* in New York.

Recorded hits for the year included *By the Light of the Silvery Moon* and *I Wonder Who's Kissing Her Now* by Billy Murray and *I Do Like to Be Beside the Seaside* by Mark Sheridan.

BIRTHS

January 3 – Victor Borge, Danish musician and comedian.
February 9 – Carmen Miranda, Brazilian singer.
February 11 – Joseph L. Mankiewitz, US director and producer.
May 15 – James Mason, British actor.
May 30 – Benny Goodman, US jazz musician.
June 7 – Jessica Tandy, US actress.
June 14 – Burl Ives, US actor, singer and writer.
June 20 – Errol Flynn, Tasmanian actor.

September 7 – Elia Kazan, US film director.
December 9 – Douglas Fairbanks Jnr, US actor.

DEATHS

March 24 – John Synge, Irish playwright (*The Playboy of the Western World*).

Literature

Novelist H.G.Wells continued his commentary on modern society and gave away something of his turbulent personal life with two novels entitled *Tono-Bungay* and *Ann Veronica*. The first sees a science student and his uncle climbing the ranks of society after making a fortune from a worthless medicine, and includes an extramarital affair with a young feminist. In the second, the heroine matures from an innocent girl into an emancipated woman determined to share her life with a man she can never marry.

At the time of publication, the author was married to second wife Jane, but was involved in a passionate affair with feminist writer Amber Reeves, who was to have their daughter, Anna Jane, in this year.

Wells described *Ann Veronica* as a 'modern love story' but many readers were shocked by the immorality of the lead characters and the obvious similarities between Ann and Amber.

TOLSTOY'S SCAPEGOATS

The publishers of Tolstoy's anti-establishment pamphlet *Thou Shalt Not Kill* were jailed by a Tsarist court in May. However, the court chose not to prosecute the author who was highly respected around the world. His novels *War and Peace* and *Anna Karenina* were bestsellers and his religious writings had gained him a devoted following in China, India, Europe and the United States.

In Rome, the 'Keats and Shelley Memorial House' was opened in April. The house, near the 'Spanish Steps', where Keats had lived and died, became a shrine to the literary legends after a campaign started in 1903 by eight New York writers and a UK committee.

The opening, presided over by King Victor Emmanuel, was described by the *New York Times* as 'a most important literary ceremony binding America, England and Italy with the same cord of poetic sentiment'.

BIRTHS

28 February – Stephen Spender, British poet.

DEATHS

April 10 – Algernon Charles Swinburne, British poet and critic.
May 18 – George Meredith, British writer.

Architecture

TWO LONDON LANDMARKS

Central London saw the completion of two major buildings – Selfridges in Oxford Street and the Victoria and Albert Museum in Kensington. The new premises for the V&A would provide a permanent home for the collections of art and artefacts that had spent fifty years moving from one venue to the next. Queen Victoria had laid the foundation of the 'South Kensington Museum' in 1899 and, at the ceremony, the name was changed to honour the monarch and her late husband. Designed by Aston Webb, who was the winner of a competition in 1891, the exterior is a mixture of Portland stone and red brick with a distinctive tower in the centre of the front façade.

A marriage of Gothic, Classical and Renaissance architecture, the main entrance features narrow arches and slim columns while the tower is reminiscent of the monarch's crown, topped with the allegorical figure of *Fame,* with its starburst halo, by Edouard Lanteri. Statues of eminent British artists stand between the uppermost windows on the four-storey building: Prince Albert and Queen Victoria stand regally above the entrances. The interior, with four levels of galleries, and the staircases are predominantly marble.

The new museum was opened by the King and Queen on June 26.

In the West End, the new Selfridges store not only ushered in a new era in shopping but also in retail architecture. The first large store to be purpose-built in London, the massive steel-framed building was designed by Chicago's leading architect Daniel Burnham and was built in several stages. The final phase in the planning, a massive tower to be erected on top of the store, was never completed. The style is classical and design includes several sculptures, including the *Queen of Time* riding on a ship of commerce over the entrance.

When the store opened in March, there was no Selfridge's sign, as owner Gordon Selfridge assumed that shoppers would recognise his magnificent building on sight.

Art

BIRTH OF BACON

Francis Bacon was born in Dublin to the English racehorse trainer Eddy and his wife Winnie, on October 28. The family moved between Ireland and England for several years before settling in London just before the First World War.

In 1929, Francis set himself up as a furniture designer and began to paint in oils in his spare time. His initial work was heavily influenced by Pablo Picasso, but the 1940s saw him move towards surrealism and eventually settle with the nightmarish visions of tortured figures which were to gain him recognition in the 1950s.

In May 2007, Bacon's *Study From Innocent X* smashed the record for

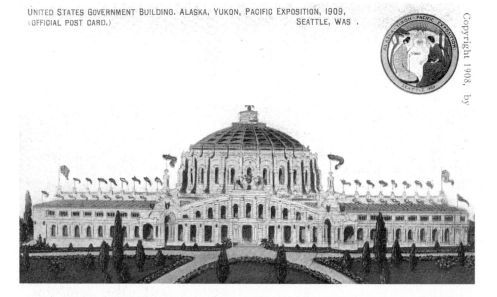

The Alaska-Yukon-Pacific Exposition in Seattle, Washington took place on what is now the University of Washington campus. It celebrated the development of the Pacific Northwest and 80,000 people attend its opening day on 1st June. By the time it closed in October, 3,700,000 had visited. The building work was partly funded by the state to allow the buildings to be turned into a University although poor standards meant few of the buildings lasted for long.

post-war art when it was sold for $52.7 million (£26.3 million) at Sotheby's in New York.

Works completed this year included the first version of Henri Matisse's *The Dance* and Pablo Picasso's Cubist masterpieces *Fruit Dish* and *Woman with a Fan.*

Travel and Transport

THE FLYING FRENCH

The French captured the imagination and worldwide fascination with aviation with some spectacular achievements this year.

On July 19, French aviator Hubert Latham failed in his first attempt to fly the Channel but his fellow countryman, Louis Blériot, succeeded six days later. He landed near Dover Castle 36½ minutes after taking off from Les Baraques, near Calais, to win the £1,000 prize offered by the *Daily Mail.*

Blériot, 37, flew a monoplane driven by a three-cylinder engine, attached to a two-bladed propeller.

The Channel flight had been the goal of three of Europe's top aviators this summer, Blériot, Hubert Latham and Charles count de Lambert – who spectacularly flew over the Eiffel Tower in front of 20,000 spectators on October 19.

There had been other successes for France earlier in the year. On May 20, Paul Tissandier made the first officially recognised world speed record for an aeroplane in a Wright biplane, achieving 34 mph.

French aviator Louis Blériot became the first person to fly over the French Channel, winning the £1,000 prize offered by *The Daily Mail.*

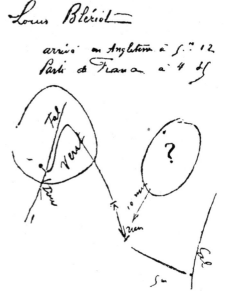

Triumphant Louis Blériot posing with his wife for photographers after his landing at Dover.

The simple sketch which Blériot drew after landing to show his route from Calais to Dover. The translation reads, 'Arrived in England at 5.12, left France at 4.35'. The circle with a question mark and the word 'rien' (meaning 'nothing'), shows where the aviator got lost en route.

The following month Blériot became the first to carry two passengers in his plane.

Later in the year, on August 27, Henri Farman made the longest aeroplane flight when he covered 111 miles in a closed circuit during the first international air race meeting at Reims in France.

But tragedy struck on September 7 when Eugène Lefebvre crashed and died while testing a Wright Model A aeroplane. He was the first pilot to die at the controls of his plane.

Elise Deroche, better known under her self-awarded title of Baronne de Laroche, made her first solo flight on October 22. She was an actress and aviator and the first woman to win her fixed-wing pilot's licence.

BIRTH OF BUGATTI CAR

Italian automobile designer Ettore Bugatti set up a factory in France this year where he built his first car. He went on to invent, design and produce a variety of models which ranged from racing cars to luxury limousines.

Toys

BIRTH OF TWO MAJOR TOY COMPANIES

The British company, Palitoy, grew out of a plastics firm, established by Alfred Edward Pallett in Leicestershire in 1909, which produced celluloid and fancy goods.

It produced its first doll in 1925 and the company subsequently became one of the country's leading toy manufacturers with popular products such as Action Man, Tiny Tears, Pippa, Care Bears and Star Wars figures.

The A. C. Gilbert Company, which was to become one of the largest toy companies in the world, was also founded this year.

Gilbert, who was from Oregon, USA, attended Yale Medical School and helped pay for his tuition by performing as a magician.

He had a childhood fascination with magic tricks and he founded a company, Mysto Manufacturing, which sold magic kits for children. In 1909, he finished medical school but decided to expand his budding toy business rather than practice as a doctor.

Gilbert was inspired whilst on a train journey, looking out the window and seeing workmen positioning and riveting steel beams into place as a tower for an electric power-cable.

He decided to create a children's construction kit with small metal beams, holes for bolts and an assembly of screws, pulleys, gears and eventually even engines. Although the Meccano Company was already selling a similar kit, Gilbert's 'Erector Set' was different in that the steel beams were bent into a 90-degree angle so that four of them connected together would form a sturdy square support.

Gilbert began selling the 'Mysto Erector Structural Steel Builder' in 1913, backed by the first major American ad campaign for a toy; it became hugely popular. Over successive years a variety of sets were produced, with different components, that would delight generations of children for years to come.

Sport

HAMPDEN PARK RIOT

One of the most notorious crowd incidents in football history occurred on April 17 at Hampden Park after the Scottish Cup Final replay between fierce rivals Celtic and Rangers.

Both games were drawn, and at the end of the second match the 60,000 spectators, who were expecting extra time, were angered when it was announced that another replay would be arranged.

There had been rumours that the Scottish Football Association had been fixing Cup ties in a bid to ensure maximum income from replays. Now this simmering resentment fuelled a riot as hundreds of fans, from both sides, swarmed onto the pitch.

Stones were thrown at the mounted police, goalposts pulled up and used as battering rams on the turnstiles and a bonfire was made out of the smashed wooden barricades.

The fire brigade arrived but were also repelled by stones and had their hoses cut. Around 100 people, mostly police and fireman, were injured before the rioters finally moved off after around two and a half hours.

Both clubs petitioned the SFA to have the tie abandoned, and so nobody won the cup this year.

SPORT OF KINGS

King Edward VII became the first monarch to own a Derby winner, although he had had two successes in the race when he was the Prince of Wales.

His horse, Minoru, received a rapturous reception when he returned to the unsaddling enclosure.

The Home

TOWN PLANNING

The planning ideas of Ebenezer Howard, successfully realised in Letchworth Garden City and Hampstead Garden Suburb by architect Raymond Unwin, were made an official policy with the 1909 Town Planning Act. Aiming to 'abolish, reconstruct and prevent the slum,' the act envisaged 'the home healthy, the house beautiful, the town pleasant, the city dignified and the suburb salubrious'.

Furthermore, it stated that town planning schemes must take into account 'proper sanitary conditions, amenity and convenience in connection with the laying out and use of the lane and of any neighbouring lands'.

Back-to-back housing, common in industrial cities, would no longer be allowed and houses had to be built to satisfy certain standards and regulations. Although the act could do nothing about the existing town centres, it was a landmark that legalised the growing view that planning homes was not merely about sanitation, facilities and structure, but about the pleasantness of the homeowners' environment.

As the decade drew to a close, the city slums were not entirely a thing of the past, but better housing for all was firmly on the political agenda and those bent on reform were winning the day.

THE WONDER OF WOOLIES

A new store in Liverpool was set to have a huge impact on the lives of the least well off. American businessman F.W.Woolworth opened his first UK outlet in Church Street on Friday November 5 although, in keeping with American tradition, no sales were made on the first day. Instead shoppers were offered free tea and entertained by a brass band as they perused the displays.

According to a reporter from the *Liverpool Courier*, the premises were 'thronged the whole time they were open, many no doubt attracted by the novel character of the business transacted. 6d is the highest price charged for any single article in the establishment, but the variety of articles obtainable is infinite'.

The store offered a huge array of china, glassware, household goods, children's clothes, paper patterns, materials, stationery, pots and pans: all at a knock down price. Most items were either 6d or 3d with some lines just a penny.

Children could choose a mixture from huge china troughs of sweets, like today's pick 'n' mix counters, and tin toys were also available.

The refreshment room on the first floor proved such a hit that F.W.Woolworth decided to introduce the idea in his US stores. For the first year, the Liverpool branch served pots of tea for free, to encourage shoppers to stay and browse as they were unaccustomed to spending time on leisurely shopping.

Over the next five years 43 Woolworths stores opened in the UK and there are now over 800 branches.

The Changing Role of Women

HUNGRY FOR VOTES

While serving a sentence for militant action, Marion Wallace Dunlop decided to go on a hunger strike, opening a new chapter in Suffragette tactics. Although Dunlop was a member of the Women's Social and Political Union, the Pankhursts had not sanctioned self-starvation, but it was soon to become a common method of protest for the 'political prisoner..' Marion Dunlop was released after 91 hours of her hunger strike, on the grounds of ill health.

However many of those who followed her in her actions were not so fortunate. In September, the Government began to tackle the problem by force-feeding the hunger strikers – a brutal procedure which involved them being held down and fed through a tube, forcibly inserted into the nose.

In response to a question by Labour MP James Keir Hardie, on September 28, the Home Office was forced to confirm that ladies in Birmingham's Winson Green Prison had been treated in this way in order to prevent them from harming themselves through self-starvation.

Two weeks later, a High Court ordered an inquiry into the procedure as the result of an action brought by suffragette Laura Ainsworth, who had been force-fed in Winson Green. After three days without eating, Mrs Ainsworth had been held down while prison workers attempted to feed her orally and then insert a nasal tube, which was blocked by a previous injury.

'I was raised into sitting position and a tube about two feet long was produced,' she stated. 'My mouth was prised open with what felt like a steel instrument. I felt a choking sensation and a cork gag was placed between my teeth to keep my mouth open. It was a horrible feeling altogether.'

Reacting to a statement by Home Secretary Herbert Gladstone that the intake of nourishment in this way was not unpleasant, George Bernard Shaw wrote a letter to *The Times* issuing a dinner invitation.

He promised that the Fabian Society would provide Gladstone with, 'The rarest wines and delicacies . . . regardless of expense.' He added, 'The only condition we shall make is that Mr Herbert Gladstone shall partake through the nose; and that a cinematograph machine be at work at the time registering for the public satisfaction the waterings of his mouth, the smackings of his lips, and other unmistakable symptoms of luxurious delight.'

In fact, several suffragettes died as a result of force-feeding before the policy was changed in 1913.

In London, a court ruling declared that women had no legal right to a divorce, even from a husband who had deserted them. A study showed that a third of the capital's workforce were women – over 200,000 of whom were in domestic service.

Science

BLOOD AND ACID

Austrian biologist and physician Karl Lansteiner categorised four basic blood groups as A, B, AB, and O.

Between 1901 and 1903, Lansteiner had discovered that during a blood transfusion from human to human, different foreign bloods tended to clump and cause shock or jaundice. During this research, he proposed that the paternity of a child could be determined because the characteristics of blood groups are inherited.

Danish biochemist Soren Sorensen invented the PH scale for measuring acidity. Sorensen studied chemistry at Copenhagen and was director of chemistry at the Carlsberg Laboratory from 1901.

Conclusion

IN HIS 1909 report, *Liberalism and the Social Problem*, Winston Churchill outlined the mammoth task which the Liberal government faced and warned that failure to bring about social reform would end in class war:

We are at a crossways. If we stand in the happy-go-lucky way, the richer classes ever growing in wealth and in number, and ever declining in responsibility, the very poor remain plunged or plunging even deeper into hopeless helpless misery, then I think there is nothing before us but savage strife between class and class.

For some, the new century was a time of despair, high unemployment, bloodshed and the threat of war with better guns, faster ships and growing enmity between the royal families.

The reforms of the decade were yet to have a dramatic effect on poverty but the attitude towards the poorer classes had changed since the dark Victorian days. The Edwardians had begun to see that the crushing lives in the slum or the workhouse should not be inevitable, but were a problem that should be eradicated.

The People's Budget of 1909 reflected the new thinking on the working classes, by advocating large taxes on the super-rich to pay for the reforms necessary to ease the burden of the poor.

The constitutional crisis arising from the Budget saw the Liberals returned a year later, but without a majority, meaning a coalition had to be formed with Labour MPs in order to pass further measures.

But by 1910, the groundwork had been laid for better housing, more employment and help for those who were unable to work at all. Old Age Pensions provided a better standard of living for those at one end of the age range while, at the other, the lives of poverty-stricken children had already improved immeasurably, with free education, school meals, medical checks and stricter laws on child labour.

The Suffragettes' struggle had increased in intensity, with hunger strikes

For others, the new century and a new king promised hope and excitement, developments in transport and industry – cars, airships, aeroplanes, radios. The world was becoming smaller, the South Pole was in sight and politicians, such as Randolph Churchill (pictured) saw a glorious future for the British Empire.

and campaigns of violence, but the movement was still a long way from achieving its goals. The following decade would see the death of Emily Davison, who threw herself under the King's Horse at the Epsom Derby in 1913, and a suspension of drastic action due to World War One.

The end of the first decade of the Twentieth Century was also the end of the Edwardian era. Edward VII died on May 6, 1910, from pneumonia, and was succeeded by his son George V. With Germany already stock-piling warships, the loss of the King, who had maintained great diplomatic ties with his cousin Kaiser Wilhelm, meant that relations in Europe were to become more strained.

Although the reforms during Edward's reign were considerable, it was the Great War of 1914–1918 which was to bring about much greater social change. With the majority of young men fighting, and armament factories stretched to the limit, there was a huge boost in employment. The role of women changed dramatically, with many working in factories and hospitals or devoting their time to voluntary work, and 80,000 serving in non-combatant military positions.

The First World War was to dominate the new decade and alter every aspect of life in the UK. Almost a million British and Commonwealth servicemen died in the conflict and, although it was dubbed 'the war to end all wars', it would not be the last time that Britain and Europe faced such devastation.

Reference Works

SOME OF THE SOURCES USED IN THIS BOOK ARE LISTED BELOW:

A History of Everyday Things in England Vol IV 1851–1914 by Marjorie & C.H.B. Quennell. Pub. B.T. Batsford.

The Edwardian House by Helen Long. Pub. Manchester University Press.

History of Twentieth Century Fashion by Elizabeth Ewing. Pub. B.T. Batsford.

Twentieth Century Fashion 1900–20 'Linen & Lace' by Sue Mee. Pub. Heinemann Library.

Finding Out About Edwardian Britain by Michael Rawcliffe. Pub. B.T. Batsford.

The Edwardians by Christopher Martin. Pub. Wayland

Chronicle of the 20th Century. Pub. Longman.

The Macmillan Encyclopedia. Pub. Macmillan.

Webster's Dictionary of Famous People. Pub. Websters.

New York Times online.

National Archives website

. . . . and a great many more websites, too numerous to mention.

Index